Believing in Obama

Essays from the Historic 2008 Election and Insights for 2012

By

Patricia Wilson-Smith

First published by 1534 Press 06/01/2012

ISBN: 0-9772250-7-0 (e-Book)

ISBN: 0-9772250-6-2 (Hard Cover)

ISBN: 0-9772250-8-9 (Paperback)

For information concerning special discounts on bulk purchases contact 1534 Press at 404-692-5251.

Printed in the United States of America

Atlanta, GA

Acknowledgements

This book is dedicated to my son David, who at 15 finally understands why I sleep with my laptop; and to all of the people who have toiled incessantly to help me realize my dream of publishing this book – my agent, Michael Andrews of Spotlight Entertainment and the other members of my support team, Pamela Kohn and Cheryle Harrison – I love you guys. Thank you to another David, who is one of my greatest fans and constant inspirations – David Hudson. But most of all, I dedicate this book to my 81-year-old mother, Ada Mae Roby, who was convinced that this nation was not ready to elect an African-American president, and who since the time of his election beat back a cancer so aggressive, she was written off by her doctors. Mema – you're my hero, my strength, and my favorite Black Woman for Obama!

Contents

Introduction

On November 4th, 2008, the United States of America turned a dramatic corner in its history by electing Barack Obama its first African-American President – a victory in part made possible by an amazing volunteer corps that worked tirelessly on his behalf.

It was after reading "The Audacity of Hope" that *I* decided to join the ranks of those volunteers; among other things, the book opened my eyes for the very first time to America's standing in the world, and to what the Bush Administration had done to so completely destroy it. It made me want to know more, understand more, and so like many volunteers at the time, I jumped at the opportunity to become truly engaged in the campaign, and doing so changed my perspective on politics forever.

You see, before the Obama campaign I had never worked actively for any political candidate at any level of government; I had no real understanding of the electoral process, and I had never dreamt that I could one day participate in a national party's convention. I was myself one of the heretofore unengaged electorate that Barack Obama shook out of their collective political slumber and dared to get involved. And get involved I did.

I raised funds, phone banked, and organized here in my home state of Georgia; I canvassed and helped to feed volunteers in South Carolina; I helped run a volunteer effort in Texas, and drove vans of supporters to neighboring states; I also launched a website, BlackWomenForObama.org, and began to blog until my hands ached. The website spawned a national organization, represented in 25 states, with members that eventually donated or raised over $50,000 dollars in the name of BWFO for the campaign, and worked tirelessly behind the scenes until the day he was elected. In the process I learned more about how our democracy works, and why my role in it is so important; I learned more than I ever thought I could.

I have often been asked about the website - "why BLACK Women for Obama, and not just WOMEN for Obama?" The answer to that question lies within the context of the 2008 Primary race itself. I had decided to get involved in a big way when I realized how important the black female vote would be during a primary that pitted Obama against Hillary Clinton. From the start, the question that many were asking was "How will black women vote in this election?" Many were convinced that as a voting bloc we would be torn, as if we were only capable of evaluating a candidate based on either gender or race. I realized then that black women in this country had little to no voice as it related to presidential elections, and that a change was needed. I vowed to spend as much time as I could letting the world know that there was at least one ordinary black woman who fervently believed in Senator Obama almost from the beginning, and dedicated myself to providing a forum for others like me who couldn't be heard over the cry of support for the Clintons that was coming from the Black community at the time.

It was absolutely indescribable, watching this nation have a two-year long dialog on gender and race, and its place in presidential politics, along with every other nail-biting, news-grabbing controversy – and what a remarkable growth experience for me! Watching, and learning as America's emotions ran the gambit - from disinterest at first, when so many who'd never heard of then Senator Obama struggled to even pronounce his name, to disbelief post-Iowa over the transformation that took place when it became apparent that mainstream

America really had voted for him. Suddenly, African-Americans had our first really viable black candidate, and a shot at making history!

Now it's 2012, and though President Obama's re-election bid is less exciting, less historic than in 2008, it's even more critical. The country is still fighting its way out of the cacophonous ditch that eight years of Bush Administration policies left us in - there's still so much work to do. Though I was forced to go on with my life after President Obama was elected in 2008, it's now time to pick up the mantle again, and declare that after four years, after all of the partisan dueling, the political ups and downs that President Obama has faced, I am still proudly a Black Woman for Obama – and what better way to do that than by looking back at my first experience, and doing my small part to remind anyone who will listen of how incredible the feeling of hope was back then, how awe-inspiring our collective anticipation. My hope is that in doing so, some will be reminded of why it's so important to continue to lend their voices to the process, and others will be inspired to put an Obama 2012 bumper sticker over the old '08 version and re-declare their support.

For the most part, this book wrote itself over the course of the two years during which I first volunteered with the Obama campaign. I've compiled these writings and essays for those who like me, love and support President

Barack Obama, and want to reminisce about the challenges, the twists, and the turns of the 2008 presidential election, or who might just want to know what it was like to be a soldier on the ground with the Obama Campaign. In any case, this book recounts my time as a volunteer, some of my experiences and many of my observations through what turned out to be one of the longest and most exciting presidential races in our nation's history, and two of the most exciting years of my otherwise ordinary life.

Barack Who?

It was August 2nd, 2007, and I'd just spent the day preparing for a business trip, and of course, because I am a black woman, I had to take a trip to my local nail salon.

I spent an excruciating three hours with a wonderful Vietnamese shop owner name Mary, who is meticulous in all she does, and extremely talkative. As a matter of fact, her talkativeness (Hmmmm, is that a word?) is infectious, and before I and the other ladies in the salon knew it, we had a brisk conversation going about absolutely nothing at all.

I know an opportunity when I see one. I pulled out my Black Women For Obama business cards in dramatic fashion and offered it to the lady to my right (let's call her "Lady #1"). I asked Lady #1 in a way that I hoped didn't sound too harassing, "So who are you supporting this election year for President?" She was very nice, and admitted openly that that was not her "thing". I would need to speak to her husband.

I gave this woman my best spiel about how black women have to become part of the political process, and why it was so important in this election year more than any other. She listened intently, and then said, "Wow, my husband is going to LOVE talking to you! That's his thing, ya know, the whole political thing!" Oy.

Next, I jumped from my seat and handed a card to a very nice, quiet, unassuming lady who was seated in a salon spa chair having her feet worked on vigorously by a perky salon worker (let's call her "Lady #2"). As I stood in front of Lady #2 and offered her my card, she asked if I was a teacher, having overheard part of my conversation with Lady #1.

"Yes, I am", I replied. "At the college level. I taught part-time for SPSU for years, and now I'm taking a break, partly so that I can help Senator Barack Obama get elected".

I waited for that glimmer of recognition, that "OH!" expression to cross her face, any gesture or sign that might tell me that she knew who I was talking about. Instead, what she said next nearly floored me:

"Oh. I...don't know who that is."

"You don't know who *I* am??!?" I asked, because that wouldn't have been that surprising. After all, I had just walked in the salon door a half hour earlier.

(Note: I intentionally misunderstood. It was a coping mechanism.)

"Uh, well, no I don't know who *you* are of course, but I don't know who E-shack Bomamba is either..."

"B-Barack Obama. Barack Obama", I said through clinched teeth. "Do you know who Hillary Clinton is?"

She nodded. And I think you get the point.

What I came to discover in that short time that I had been working to get Black Women For Obama off the ground is that (at the time) scant few black women gave even a second thought to the political process. Many of us, too busy and severely taxed just trying to keep food on the table and our kids on the right path, get our political educations from 30 second sound bites on the nightly or 24-hour news channels. And so, so many of us got the magical message back in the nineties that Bill Clinton was the greatest thing since sliced bread, (and he was close), that now we're willing to take Hillary on the strength of her association with him.

This is not good, and it's one of the main reasons why a Hillary Clinton presidency doesn't sit well with me. I don't believe that a lot of people are electing Hillary; I think they really want to RE-elect Bill, and though I am a huge fan of Bill Clinton, I feel very strongly that he and Hillary have had their time.

The style of politics that our most recent presidents have engaged in has failed black women. In our communities, black women are having babies out of wedlock at the rate of 70%. Aids is ravaging our sisters, opportunities are still not equal, and the United States is slipping further and further behind other developed nations when it comes to the quality of education we provide our children. All of this while politicians bat wildly at each other like two 8-year old school girls in a playground fist-fight.

And so, I hold BWFO, and other organizations like it up as a beacon of hope to those who know we need and want something better, and even to those who may not know, like Lady #2 from the salon. The bottom line is, the privilege of voting means nothing if we don't educate ourselves on who the candidates are, and where they stand on the issues. We *have* to make informed decisions about how we're going to spend our precious votes, and not even knowing WHO comprises the field of candidates in the party we blindly support is like ordering the first thing you see from a restaurant menu without reviewing your choices and then bitching when your meal is not to your satisfaction.

Black women - if we don't make our voices heard now, we will NOT be heard later!

If you care about moving this great nation in the right direction, find some organization to get involved with that will help you become a part of the political happenings around you. We all owe it to ourselves, and the mothers, daughters and friends we love so much to not let them off the hook for not getting involved. Spread the word - this is the year of the black woman when it comes to the selection of our next President, and Black Women for Obama is leading the charge!

Camp Obama

There is nothing more gratifying than to come together with people of like minds for a common cause.

This weekend in Atlanta, a large number of Barack Obama supporters have gathered to participate in "Camp Obama", a training initiative created by the Obama campaign to introduce his many grass-root supporters all over the country to the tenets of his campaign, and to train them on canvassing, manning phone banks, and other community organizing methods. Camps like the one going on this weekend in the ATL have already taken place in cities all over the country, including Phoenix, AZ, Boise, ID and St. Louis, MO.

When I first heard about Camp Obama coming to Atlanta, I signed up immediately. As a staunch Obama supporter and founder of BWFO, I felt it was my duty to get all of the information available on how to be most effective for the Senator's campaign. I made application online like everyone else, and received a call from the Southeast Field Coordinator several days later. I was put through a less-than-arduous interview, and then eventually informed that I had been accepted into the camp (I have no idea how many people were denied acceptance, but I'm having fun pretending that the number was in the thousands!).

When I signed up for the group mailing list to officially accept my spot in the Camp, I didn't know that I would soon be inundated with enthusiastic emails from people from around the country who were just as excited as I was about the prospect of learning more about the inner-workings of the Obama Campaign. I mean, these people were fired up, and clearly ready to roll up their sleeves and get down to the business of getting the Senator elected, and from the sound of their emails, they are more than passionate and driven enough to do just that!

People like Freeman McNeal (not the football player), a political consultant who came in all the way from Cincinnati for Camp Obama. Or Cherry Vincent, who made the trip down from Norfolk, Virginia. Not to mention the legions of people from the local Atlanta area, many of whom have generously offered their time and assistance to the out-of-towners to make their trip to Camp Obama an easier one - the spirit of camaraderie is flowing like, well, things that flow, and it's infectious and really amazing!

Yep - there's hope in the air people, and it makes you do crazy things. Not wanting to be out done, I contacted the National Campaign and offered sleeping space in my home for anyone that needs it, and as of this writing, I have two wonderful total strangers bunking with me (both of whom are last-named King - eerie coincidence, or cosmic karma? I'll let you decide). Despite what the media, the polls, or even your unenlightened next door neighbor might tell you, there is a powerful movement a-foot and there is more than enough reason for hope, as David Plouffe, Senator Obama's brilliant campaign manager pointed out in an email on Friday that went out to Obama supporters:

"In mid-September 2003, a national poll put the eventual nominee John Kerry behind Howard Dean -- and both of them behind the frontrunner in the polls, Joe Lieberman. Then Kerry won the Iowa caucus and the New Hampshire primary, and that momentum carried him all the way to the nomination. The lesson: early polls don't mean a thing and momentum in crucial early-state contests will win the Democratic nomination."

Senator Obama's campaign so far has been a study in what is possible when ordinary citizens band together. It is so very important that those of us who understand the importance of this election and the impact that an Obama presidency could have, continue to brush past the polls, the negativity, and the media speculators, and do all that we can to make it a reality. It would be SO easy to tell ourselves that the naysayers are right, that Senator Obama's candidacy is a long-shot - the problem is, we know what so many other people will soon know - that not only are Senator Obama's plans for undoing the mess that the last few administrations have made sound and sensible, but they're also good for all Americans, and good for the world. Senator Obama will invigorate the electorate, bring fresh ideas to old problems, and invoke a renewed spirit of cooperation in a way that recent administrations have failed to do.

And so, all of the hopeful, buoyant men and women who previously were just emails and voices over the telephone have descended on Morris Brown College this weekend to report for duty. It will be our jobs as residents of the Southeast to get the training we need to make an impact in the state where we're needed most right now - South Carolina. Black women for Obama has already established a chapter in South Carolina, and we're committed to making an impact across the nation as the Obama army marches on through the first round of primaries.

With scant few months until the important first primaries, we are definitely, smack dab in the middle of

"The Countdown to Change". To quote a beloved musical legend, I'm ready to make it "do what it do" - are you?

The Mis-education of Oprah Winfrey

The last thing I wanted to do on a cozy Sunday evening here at home with my son staring over my shoulder is write an article that I'm certain some will view as a pot-shot at one of the most beloved women of the modern age, but I just can't help myself. By now, it is common knowledge that just recently the *Oprah Winfrey Leadership Academy for Girls* opened its doors to 450 deserving South African girls who were hand-selected by Oprah herself. The new luxury facility which boasts a beauty salon, computer and science labs, and modern dorm rooms, is situated on 52 acres in a remote community south of Johannesburg South Africa.

It was only *just now* that I discovered what Oprah said in a recent Newsweek article, in which she explained why she chose to build the state-of the art campus for the children of South Africa rather than for needy school kids here in the United States:

22

"I became so frustrated with visiting inner-city schools that I just stopped going. The sense that you need to learn just isn't there," she says. "If you ask the kids what they want or need, they will say an iPod or some sneakers. In South Africa, they don't ask for money or toys. They ask for uniforms so they can go to school."

Source: http://www.Racialicious.com, 01/03/07

As a middle-aged black woman who grew up in the inner-cities of the Midwest, my sensibilities are offended by Oprah's assessment on so many levels that it's hard to put it into words; however, despite my discomfort at questioning the actions of a woman who is so beloved, and who has clearly done so much for so many, I have to try, because *this time* Oprah's sincere but misguided evaluation of the wants and desires of inner-city youths proves once and for all that being rich and influential does not always translate to being socially or even culturally responsible.

First a point of clarification – I have been and will likely always be a *huge* fan of Oprah Winfrey's. Her philanthropic activities throughout the United States and the world are legendary, and I for one believe that history will one day portray her as a modern day saint not at all unlike the late Mother Theresa. Her rags to riches story, the ultimate self-made woman tale is an ever-present inspiration to me as a black woman, and I would defend her right to spend the money that she has worked so hard to make in any forum. No - the problem here is not how she has chosen to spend her money, but how in doing so she has irresponsibly cast an unfair light on a population of defenseless and in most cases underprivileged children.

Here's the thing: if children in inner-city schools are not getting the message that their educations should be the most important thing in their lives, there are many reasons why. Conversely, if there is a sense that education is more important than iPods and sneakers in South African schools, there are also reasons why, and it is these reasons that Ms. Winfrey seems to have completely disregarded in making her very careless remark.

Firstly, and most obviously, children in inner-city schools, even in areas where the tax base cannot even ensure decent plumbing in their school buildings all have access to one thing – the almighty-fantasy-generator we call *television*. That purveyor of all things pleasurable and lofty, that 'spewer' of dream images, chocked full of beautiful and flawless people - men, women, boys and girls with perfect hair, bodies, and teeth seemingly all carrying brand spanking new iPods as they run effortlessly through some picturesque suburban neighborhood somewhere in the latest high-fashion (and high-priced) sneakers without breaking a sweat. That television. Most inner-city kids have these images force fed to them day in and day out. Is it any wonder that our children would come off as mindless iPod or Air Jordan zombies when asked by the richest woman in the world what their fondest wish might be? Can they honestly be blamed if they can't resist the constant barrage of instant gratification messages targeted at them on a daily basis by the media? To add more fuel to the ridiculousness of Oprah's statement, the fact simply can't be ignored that many of the mind-numbing, glossy, you-gotta-have-this now ads that permeate the free-viewing airwaves are coming from some of the very corporations who produce some of the products whose colossal advertising budgets have made a great portion of Oprah Winfrey's immense fortune possible.

Secondly, Oprah's is an absolutely unfair comparison. In a nation where the black children are only a generation removed from the ravages of the Apartheid struggle, and where as recently as the early 1990's the entire nation of blacks was routinely suppressed from participating in the national economy, it seems Pollyanna to believe that the day to day wants of the nation's children would have yet evolved beyond an equal education and the bare necessities that so many of the girls selected to go to the school have to do without on a regular basis. Oprah, of course they don't aspire to fancy shoes and iPods – do they even have computers? Internet access? I admit I don't know the answer, but it's a good bet that Apple's market penetration into the outer provinces of South Africa probably leaves a bit to be desired.

Finally, it is patently irresponsible for a woman of her broad influence to make such a sweeping statement in the media about a population of children that are so in need of everyone's help. The sad fact of reality is that when anyone in the media says *inner-city*, most Americans hear *minorities*, and the low-income minorities in this country are having a difficult enough time as it is keeping the money flowing into their public schools, and can at this point still only expect to get a second-rate education for their children at best. I literally cringe at the thought of the legion of middle and upper-class soccer moms who comprise Oprah's core audience, who upon reading her comments will all be out there clicking their tongues at 'those poor misguided inner-city youths, who don't even have enough sense to value education over material things' as if rich kids are any different. Putting that notion out there at a time when some seem to be working overtime to widen racial divides is just plain reckless.

The icing on the cake? The new Leadership Academy's website (http://www.oprahwinfreyleadershipacademy.org) asks you to make a donation to continue to support the school. What?!? Now don't get me wrong - there's nothing wrong with wanting to help these children at all, and again, I acknowledge with all the respect in the world the great work that Oprah Winfrey has done with her Angel Network charity and so many others, but I'm not going to send one thin dime to South Africa to make sure that those students have hair gel in their new luxury salon when I know there are students here in the United States using text books that were written in the nineteen-sixties.

But - I can't help but wonder what would happen if Oprah erected a website called "SupportAmericasSchools.com" to solicit donations for *our* public schools, complete with a gorgeous photo of her surrounded by the many children who live in areas where their schools have been abandoned, forgotten, and left to fall into disrepair. I'm guessing that without writing a single check herself, if she wanted to, she could start a flow of money into America's public school systems that could make a real difference for those communities in need, and perhaps go a long way towards the goal of providing equal education for all children here at home, because Oprah wields just that much influence here. And I say, if there is a chance that she could make a difference here then she should, because I've always been told that to whom much is given, much is expected. I've also always been taught that charity begins at home. If the most powerful black woman in the world can't see the problems inherent in America's education system, how we got here, and why our children might need a little help with their perspectives and setting priorities, well, then as a society, we're in big trouble.

Ms. Winfrey, with all due respect, it is okay to acknowledge that our kids have issues and need our help, but it's not okay to 'stop going' as you put it. If our kids don't have the sense that they need to learn, then it is the job of every adult in this nation to give it to them, including yours. But it is also not Oprah's job to do alone. By not doing the work ourselves to build a solid foundation for our children's futures here at home, we're all ensuring that a nation that has always been generous to a fault with giving to those in need abroad might one day not be as well equipped to do so.

If you want to help even in a small way, contact a local public school in your area and make a donation to their PTA, or volunteer. Do something. Do anything. But don't give up on our children, because we just can't afford to.

Commas for Obama: We Pause for Thought

I often surf the web when I have nothing better to do, and because the focus of my efforts for the Obama campaign has been on getting the word out to the black community, I often visit social networking sites for African Americans in search of opportunities to answer questions, debunk myths, and refute incorrect claims regarding the Senator and his campaign.

Today, I came across what could best be described as a sincere cry for help from a young man on one of the most popular social networking sites for blacks, and it got me to thinking - what better way to start a deeper dialog on THIS site, than to seek out these cries for help anywhere I can find them and answer them!

And so today, I introduce the first installment of "Commas for Obama: We Pause for Thought", a segment that will appear as often as I can find a good question or misguided diatribe to which I feel compelled to respond. Thank you to my oldest friend in the world,

The subject of today's pause comes from BlackPlanet.com, and a 29-year-old male in Lawrenceville, GA who calls himself ONONYMOUS.

Onomymous

Male, 29, Lawrenceville, GA

"I need a good reason to vote for Obama, and please not because he is black. Honestly right now I am thinking Rudy Giuliani. I was born in New York and seen the changes he has done. If you haven't seen what he has done watch the movie *Fame* sometime and see New York how it used to be. I'm looking for what Obama is going to do for me financially. I don't care about things like universal health care, why should I? I worked my butt off to get where I am at, why should someone get the same benefits that I sacrificed for?? Iraq, Iran, the war on terror, whatever, tell me what he is going to do about the death of the middle class. Yes I am going to say I am middle class, I can afford to eat, pay my bills and have a good job, but with the way thing are going will I in the future? What's his platform?? This election is serious; we are living in a dictatorship right now. The power that the Bush government has is disgusting. He has gotten away with crimes that are unconstitutional. Give me a reason to look at Obama. I need to know that he will allow me to raise my future kids safely in this crazy world that we now live in. He is a good man, but that doesn't help my future. "

Dear ONONYMOUS:

The very reason why we should ALL take a look at Barack Obama is that we DON'T just have to vote for him because he's black!

First, just let me say that if you've narrowed your choices down to Barack Obama or Rudy Giuliani, and you need the TV show "Fame" to make your point, there's a deeper, fundamental struggle going on within you that needs to be dealt with. But not here.

Rudy Giuliani may be tough on crime, able to clean up a city, etc., but he does not in any way have the background or moral compass necessary to lead this or any other country. When it comes to morals, I wouldn't trust him to lead a deserted island, let alone the most powerful nation in the world. Besides, we've had 8 years of someone too willing to pull the trigger before he aims. We don't need another 8 years.

As for Senator Obama, I think we as black people may all be a little taken aback because we're so used to black candidates getting in the race for President who we know have absolutely no chance of winning. For a long time, I often wondered to myself WHY a Jesse Jackson or an Al

Sharpton would even bother with the hassle of throwing their hats in the ring, when they knew a snowball had a better chance in hell. I soon realized the truth - that they were sacrificing themselves in order to get the issues important to black people on the national stage. This is admirable, but ironically, this is not what the Obama campaign is about.

I became an Obama supporter after I realized that he had spent much of his time in the inner cities of Chicago, working with ministers and locals trying to rebuild neighborhoods, when he could have been off working some lucrative job somewhere. And when I realized that he had a solid reputation for reaching across the aisle to build consensus and get things done in the Senate I was sold.

Senator Obama lays out a new way of governing that is inclusive, and that seeks to bridge the gap that this nation's politicians have created over the last several years. Our government is practically immobilized; partisan bickering, scandalizing, and cow-towing to special interests have made it almost impossible for us to solve any of our country's problems, and that has to stop. The fact that this man, black, blue, or magenta could actually affect change at all should not cause us to question his "blackness", but to celebrate his viability.

I am by most measures a successful black woman, and yet I understand that I am in some ways very in the minority. Years of empty promises from manipulative politicians have done nothing to keep the spread of aids from ravaging the black females in our communities, and have done nothing to provide the opportunities that our black men so desperately need to keep our families together - that includes the Clinton years.

What Senator Obama offers, if you REALLY read everything you can about him, is a different kind of government, one in which our nation's problems are attacked head on and in a way that ensures that everyone is part of the process. He is not just waging a campaign, he's creating a movement; I have NEVER been involved in politics in any way, and getting involved with his campaign taught me what a serious mistake that was on my part. Unfortunately, it's human nature at times to have a very "American Idol" way of dealing with political issues - we don't get engaged until it's down to the last two. Well that won't work anymore - nothing about the way this country has been run over the last twenty years has done anything to make our schools safer, our elderly more cared for, or our communities more prosperous.

If you need a reason to vote for Senator Obama, and you really want to get to know how deeply philosophical his approach to changing this government is, pick up "The

Audacity of Hope" and read it from cover to cover. Reading that book opened my eyes to some major political realities, including and especially as they relate to the war in Iraq, and what the United States has tried to do in the Middle East in general. I'm almost willing to guarantee that if you read that book, and THEN read some of his speeches, you'll have a much clearer picture of the candidate, and feel better informed to make your decision come Primary Election Day.

Two Years After Katrina: If We Don't Get This Right

Two years ago last week, the levees off the shores of New Orleans succumbed to the pressure of rising waters brought on by Hurricane Katrina as it passed east of the city. It was arguably the most deadly hurricane in recent history, taking with it over 1800 lives across the Gulf Coast, and over 80 billion dollars in property.

On August 26, 2007, Senator Obama visited the First Emanuel Baptist Church in New Orleans and spoke to the members who still make their homes there. He also visited other sites in the area, places that are still in disrepair, and where entire neighborhoods are still as ravaged, waste-infested and uninhabitable as they were just days after the waters of Katrina subsided.

The pain and defeat on the faces of some of the people in the video that chronicled his visit were as heart-wrenching as the look of hope is on others. It is hard to believe that they could actually be talking about a major urban center in the richest nation in the world.

I wasn't personally impacted by Hurricane Katrina - but I know many people who were. I can't even *begin* to imagine what it must have been like for so many of those who were trapped in the homes they had worked so hard to buy, or who had to watch helplessly as their loved ones were washed away by the swiftly rising flood waters. The horror of it defies description. More horrible still was our government's criminally slow response to the tragedy, and the harshness with which those who would prefer to turn a blind eye to the poverty and hopelessness that was evident in the inner cities of New Orleans even *before* Katrina, judged its victims.

No sooner than the government began to distribute aid to the victims of the hurricane, the stories about how survivors were spending money began to pop up all over the media like rotten daisies. Stories of people buying electronics, jewelry, blowing money in casinos - the media hammered on these people day after day, until they got close to convincing Americans that these people were not victims of a horrendous natural disaster, or of generations of impoverished conditions, but some strange population of meteorological opportunists, just waiting for the next natural disaster to strike so that they could dupe the government out of a couple of grand to buy their next big-ticket item. They got close to convincing some. But not me.

See, I happen to believe that if you or I had been living in the conditions that many of those who were virtually abandoned during the half-hearted rescue efforts found themselves in pre-Katrina, and someone handed either of us a small financial windfall, it would probably be hard for *us* not to give in to the temptation and fulfill some small dream of a new gadget, or a trip to some place we thought we'd never see - even at our own peril. For many Katrina survivors, it was more money than they had ever seen at one time in their lives. Do I condone the way that many of them foolishly squandered the money meant to help sustain them? Of course not, but I definitely understand why they did it.

There is a much deeper story here than just the marking of a horrific anniversary - there are still so many people displaced, with no place to call home; so many who lost everything that they had worked a lifetime to build, who after paying into expensive insurance premiums year after year, decade after decade, were told that their policies would not cover their losses. Can you imagine? So not only do you no longer have a place to live, you're stuck paying a mortgage for a house that's nothing more than a pile of rubble, and your government has cruelly turned its back on you and said "we've helped enough". Ludicrous.

Senator Obama understands that there is something very wrong in all this. During his recent visit to New Orleans, he was surrounded by local leaders, and residents of one of the neighborhoods in New Orleans still struggling to recover. When asked by one woman who could hardly contain her sorrow, whether or not he would forget about New Orleans after he left, he said, "If we don't get this right, it will be a symbol of what kind of country we are. [It will say that] we as a nation have forgotten to look out for one another." And then he pledged to fight for New Orleans, no matter *what* happened in the upcoming Presidential election.

The fact that I have no doubt in my mind that Senator Obama means what he says, and will work and follow through on his promise to the woman in the video is why I support his candidacy so fervently. Senator Obama has walked with the down-trodden, and dined with heads of state, and yet his ability to keep his eye on those who America would forget is what makes him different than any of the other candidates in this election, Democrat or Republican.

If you want to do something to help the victims of Katrina who are still in need of aid, go to the American Red Cross website. You can read a special report on their response to Katrina and other recent hurricanes by clicking. The other thing you can do? Encourage others to cast a vote for Senator Obama, a man who has worked first-hand to organize communities and bring people together to find solutions to problems. With a President Obama in the White House, we're all assured of a chance at a brighter future.

Is Senator Obama Black Enough?

CNN.com reported recently that the world was almost spared yet another question about whether or not Senator Barack Obama is 'black enough' during the National Association of Black Journalists' Convention held this week in Las Vegas. We were *almost* spared. Not quite.

When asked about his 'black-titude' in the myriad of previous debates, interviews and town hall meetings that have come before the NABJ convention, the Senator has delivered the same by now very well-known line that garnered applause during the CNN/YouTube debate -the one about the question of his blackness not coming up when he's trying to catch a cab. For whatever reason Byron Pitts, a national correspondent for CBS, felt it needed to be asked just one more time, as if in some way his re-phrasing of the question would shed a light on the subject that would illuminate us all with its brilliance and increased relevance.

CNN reporters describe Senator Obama as relaxed and in his element as he stood boldly in front of the room full of black journalists. That might explain why when Pitts chose to question the Senator's blackness yet AGAIN, he gave an answer that was deeper and more elucidating than any he'd given to the 'are you black enough' question before, and in a way that should put an end to the question once and for all, though only time will tell.

Senator Obama turned the question back around on the journalists in the room, and suggested (in essence) that they should ask themselves why a man who by almost every other measure clearly is black, would be questioned repeatedly about his degree of blackness merely because of his mixed heritage or because he appeals so greatly to non-blacks. The Senator pointed to his record of community organizing, his stand on the issues, etc., as evidence that he most certainly is 'black enough', and wondered aloud why that wasn't enough for some people.

His question was a rhetorical one, but I think that if it doesn't beg for an answer, it at least deserves a closer look. Our tendency as black people to ask these kinds of questions to those among us who for whatever reason have the ability to relate to people of other races and cultures is age old - that we would turn the question on the one man in our history who had what it took to become the first truly viable African American candidate for the office of the President of the United States means that collectively, we might need to start taking a look at ourselves.

I myself am not the deepest thinker in the world, and I can admit that. But I know all along I've felt a certain discomfort when I've heard the question of blackness posed to the Senator, and now after much self-introspection, I know why.

As a young black girl growing up in the seventies, I was constantly slapped in the face with my racial identity. First, I was too black, a child of desegregation, so I was indoctrinated early into the belief that in order to get a decent education, I needed to be bussed across town to a strange school full of white kids. It didn't matter what the real motives for desegregation were; the message I got back then was that I needed to be plucked out of my all-black neighborhood and school and integrated into the white world in order to have a chance at success. Before long I was being bounced from all-white school to all-white school in order to find a curriculum that was challenging enough to hold my attention. I'll never know whether or not I would have been any less successful if I'd stayed in my neighborhood schools, but I was a good student and very intelligent, and I did much more than hold my own with my new classmates.

Before I knew it, I was being called too white - a gifted student with a strong love of learning that had nothing to do with my ethnicity, but everything to do with my natural curiosity about all things academic, and a sincere desire to excel, I was soon alienated from my neighborhood friends because of the special programs I was able to participate in, and labeled someone who 'acted white' because I was comfortable in my own skin, even as I embraced new people, new experiences and new ideas.

Then - back to being too black. As an elementary school student, I won admission to an exclusive private school because I out-scored most of my school district in standardized tests. The school was so beautiful and regal that it seemed more like a castle. I spent precisely two days attending classes there before my mother received a call from the school's administration asking her what my race was, because she had neglected to fill it out on the proper forms upon my admission. A few days after that, I was released from the school because they discovered that they had already reached their quota for minority admissions before I was accepted. Too black. Back to public school.

I understand now that the intentions of those who thought that desegregating our public school systems could somehow begin to fix our racial ills were mostly honorable. I realize that what was at stake was a battle to change hearts and minds, in ways and through challenges that I was far too young to understand at the time. But while on the one hand I believed I was lucky to have the opportunity to be removed from my depressed surroundings and placed in the midst of more fortunate children in their clean schools with their new textbooks, on the other hand I begin to get a sense that my blackness was being compromised - always, always the struggle with too black, or too white.

Now, I'm a proudly strong and confident black woman, with 42 years of life under my belt to clear up my perspective. Now I know that the reality is, what it means to be black in this country has changed and was changing even back then, evolving into something much deeper than what it had been before, certainly deeper than just the school I attended, or the neighborhood I grew up in. The reality is that what it means to be black in this country this day and age defies a neat definition.

Being black in this country now means, regardless of your beginnings, you might one day be a wealthy, successful black woman, married to a white man. Being black could mean you may have been educated in all-white schools, even raised by a white family, but gone on to become a great advocate for black causes. Being black in this country means that you may have grown up in the inner-city, and been told that you had no opportunity or hope of making anything of yourself, but that you fought your way out through hard work and perseverance, maybe because you were a brilliant scientist, a really talented athlete, or a prolific writer. And being black in this country means you may have been born of a white mother, a Kenyan father, and raised in a small apartment on a beautiful Hawaiian country side. It could mean that you spent time in Indonesia, and that maybe even because of your mixed heritage, you devoted your life to the public service of all people, those less fortunate, disenfranchised, and who had no voice and needed your help, no matter what their race.

The Al Sharpton's and Jesse Jackson's of the world don't own being black any more than the Oprah Winfrey's and Bill Cosby's do, because being black in this country has come to mean so many different things, and Senator Obama knows that. His answer to Byron Pitt's question was brave, insightful, and indicative of his ability to get past the ridiculousness that threatens to demean the important process of electing our next world leader. To ask a man that has worked tirelessly in the inner-city neighborhoods of Chicago helping to rebuild communities, a man that has stood side by side with black religious leaders to solve problems in the worst neighborhoods in the city if he's 'black enough' is nothing short of ridiculous. Like Senator Obama, I think those that even dare ask that intensely stupid question seek to strip him of his blackness because they feel a certain discomfort over his bi-racial ethnicity, and are unable to relate to his culturally diverse background. Me? I consider that both those aspects of him have done a great deal to shape who he is as a man, just as my experiences as a young child worked to shape the woman I have become, for better or worse. In my mind, Senator Obama's unique life experience gives him the kind of depth of character that is needed to be a leader of inclusion. Be he black, white or some funky fuchsia color, Senator Obama has the right vision for this country, and that's all that should really matter.

But I can't help but ask the question - to those people who would withhold their support for Senator Obama because he's not black enough - it couldn't really be just about that, right? I mean, isn't he at least several shades more black than Hillary?

Commas for Obama #2

Wow.

Every once in a while, something I write actually gets someone's attention; occasionally, I even hear from someone who either totally agrees with me, or thinks I'm a raving lunatic. Some people agree with me but still think I'm a lunatic.

I have to say, however, that I was not prepared for the response I received to the "The Bill Factor" piece that appeared on the site a few days ago. So, in the spirit of fair play, and pausing for thought, I decided to share some of those responses with you, my faithful readers. So here it is, unedited, for your enjoyment!

Response #1

Yours is a well-expressed summation of the "Bill" factor in our community. Sure, I, too, voted for Bill--twice. I appreciated his closeness to our community, his comfort level with our people. We would hope that all presidents would be able to comfortably form relationships with people regardless of their race, culture, religion. We need leaders who can claim friends from all socio-economic groups. But you are right in pointing out that voting decisions must consider other factors. After all, Bush also has a lot of friends who are black, Hispanic, female, etc. Charisma aside, there are many things President Clinton did--as the leader of the Democratic Party--that I, as a progressive, did not appreciate. For examples--1. He took the party to the CENTER in an attempt to appear more REPUBLICAN fiscally. By doing so, he alienated the heart and soul, the pulse, the lifeblood of the Democratic Party--the Progressives-- those frequently unkempt activists, labor organizers, and blue-collar working people--many of whom fled to the Green Party; became unavailable when Gore's time to bat appeared. Welfare reform would have been a better idea if Clinton had had a plan for employing all the people who lost benefits so abruptly. But at the time, it was more important for him to be seen destroying the program so as not to be accused of being a tax and spend LIBERAL. He regrets this now--he has publicly admitted the error of this tactic--but the damage was done, and because of it George Dubya Bush won the White House.

2. In this same vein, he "cleansed" the party of the left/progressives and brought in his Hollywood "Golden Girls" buddies to produce & script the convention so that it looked like the Academy Awards instead of our beloved, customarily rowdy Democratic Convention. Everybody had to stay on message, and no one could admit being a Liberal. (Remember? They were so afraid Jesse Jackson was going to say something radical like "We Shall Overcome.") This was definitely not cool.

3. Personally, I liked Jocelyn Elders, his first surgeon general, whom Billary coldly dumped after she advised young people to use birth control if they were having sex. I also liked Lani Guinier--the first black woman to achieve tenure in Harvard's Law School. Billary dumped her from the nomination to Attorney General for Civil Rights after Republicans derided her as the "quota queen." Remember that? A scholar, she had researched how political districts are formed in this country and how redistricting more times than not disenfranchised minority voters. She had developed a correction for this imbalance, which infuriated the likes of Jesse Helms. Puh-lease! This is a post that Clarence Thomas, our current Supreme Court Justice (aka Anita Hill dog) held for years. Billary caved.

But, as Marshall Ganz reminded us, people vote on an emotional level most of the time. I've often tried to remind people of these facts, only to be told--"well, I liked the way she stood by her man."

As we begin engaging voters on behalf of Barack Obama, I would follow his lead and show them he is not taking their votes granted, or expecting them to vote for him because he is cute or black or white or Christian or male or female. He wants to know how he, as President, can help them improve the quality of their lives and he wants everyone who is working on his behalf to ask the voter for his or her support.

I don't know what you are finding, but I'm finding that Obama supporters are the first ones out of the gate and on the neighbor's front porch, ringing the bell. I don't see any Billary workers anywhere in the communities asking voters for anything. Come Election Day, they may remember that.

Right on!

T. McDonald

P.S. And yes, if all else fails, I, too, suggest that we can't bring back the past by electing relatives or family members to the same office; job skills are not transferable based on family or marital ties. What better example of this than Dubya? I mean, geez, folks, would you ask the spouse of your surgeon to operate on you if that surgeon died?

Response #2

Bravo for your letter-as far as I am concerned, Hillary is just not skeptical enough-namely that she failed to question two really important statements -the first being 'I did not have sex with that woman', that secured the presidency for the Republicans and, of course, failing to even read the documents and question the Bush administration's push for war against Iraq-plunging us into a disastrous and costly war. To say nothing of the mess she made of the health care reform issue. Having dealt with insurance issues related to my son's cancer and his relapse for the past five years, I can only say, if this is the wonk solution, it is ill-conceived and not humane. I believe that Senator Obama is the only candidate who can heal this country and bring us together. Hillary does not have a prayer of doing that-not a prayer! Thanks for speaking out and helping develop a dialogue for the rest of us to respond to those who prefer Billary!

Sharon

Response #3

I enjoyed reading this very interesting article and concur that Sen. Barack Obama is the best candidate to be president of the United States at this juncture in American history. Clearly, his victory would be a defining bench mark for the future. However, there are some lacunae in the analysis. First of all, as the author mentioned, Sen. Hillary Clinton is also presidential timber. In my view, to evaluate her candidacy through the prism of her husband Bill is to give her unwarranted short shrift. It may come as a surprise to some that winning the presidency requires more that getting the black vote. First of all, the black community is by no way monolithic in spite of its propensity to vote for Democratic candidates, as it should given Republican virtual disdain for the black population.

Now, candidates need to appeal to a cross section of voters beyond sectarian, religious, gender, and racial lines. This approach is sensible and practical. Failure to do so will lead to disaster for Obama at the polls. Frankly, Obama's mettle will not be assessed by his affinity to black voters but more on his ability to promote and effectuate change from which the entire citizenry will benefit.

This notion of a zero-sum game is antiquated and not useful in the times in which we now live. Further, America's prestige abroad will not necessarily be enhanced by the fact of him being a black president. Obama must show that he's capable of handling domestic issues as well and international schisms which if left unresolved can threaten the interests and security of the United States.

Obama's negritude is a given. However, he must demonstrate that he's sufficiently attuned to the difficulties facing some segments of the black community. But as president, his preoccupation should be focused across the national spectrum and be pragmatic. Symbolism is not enough. If he engages in gender and racial politics his chances of winning the presidency will be diminished.

This outcome would be a disaster for an eminently qualified candidate. As president Obama has to become a statesman and less of a parochial political figure in the trenches. Leadership and vision are key attributes, and he has them. He need not resort to divisiveness to garner votes. He should follow his natural instincts born of his unique experience and promote inclusiveness.

Earle

Obama, Jesse, and the Jena 6

If by now, you still need a reason for why I started BWFO, you need look no further than the man who was once considered one of the most important black leaders in this country - Reverend Jesse Jackson.

Earlier this week, Reverend Jackson, a self-proclaimed Obama supporter, let slip during a 45-minute one on one interview with a reporter from South Carolina's "The State" newspaper, that in not responding more strongly to the now well known "Jena 6" case in Louisiana, Senator Obama was "acting like he's white".

I shuddered when I heard this too. I'll take a moment and let your shudder die down - it'll be tough though, because it comes in waves, doesn't it?

Yes it does. So as a proud member of Black Women for Obama, and a sworn defender of the Senator, I have to respond. The problem is when I think about Jesse Jackson's latest shenanigans, the only thing that comes to my mind is - why? Why is it so easy for a man like Jesse Jackson to let such toxic words fall from his mouth about a man who is our first real hope for a President who, well, isn't white, and who has done more than what's necessarily required of him to denounce the horrible situation in Jena, Louisiana?

I'm tempted to end my musings here with a "beats the heck outta me", and a "thank you and good-nite", but I can't, because I'm genuinely puzzled. I'm confused, and yet strangely fascinated by what could have possibly motivated Jesse Jackson to say such a thing. So I am here tonight to offer up some possible theories. I welcome yours (clear throat).

Theory # 1: Jesse Jackson is the king of the political "player haters"; perhaps he simply can't stand to see another African American man get so close to something that was so unattainable for him. Sounds plausible, but then the man did endorse Senator Obama back in March of this year, so though it's theory number one, it's not the strongest.

Theory # 2: He's a secret agent and under-cover attack dog for the Clintons. This theory has legs, my friends. Jesse Jackson has been a close personal friend of the Clinton's for years. What if - just work with me for a moment - the Clinton campaign secretly hired Reverend Jackson to pretend to be an endorser of Senator Obama's, in order to get information about the inner workings of his campaign? And worse yet, what if he was really engaged by the Clintons to spout off at the mouth about the slightest gaffe the Senator might make in order to bolster support for the Clintons with blacks? I mean THINK ABOUT IT - there are still dyed-in-the-wool Jackson supporters out there who think the man's mouth is a prayer book. I'm just sayin'.

Theory # 3: The real Jesse Jackson was abducted years ago by alien life forms, who cruelly left us stuck with a talking and remarkably human-like Jesse Jackson doll with a bad micro-chip. Hmmmm.

Theory # 4: (And the more likely theory) Foot-in-Mouth-Syndrome. The glare of the national spotlight, and a tendency to deal with all issues in a trigger-happy, speak-then-think way has once again cast a gloomy cloud over Jesse Jackson's presumably well-intentioned rainbow.

I mean, are we really surprised? Has Jesse Jackson exactly shown himself to be careful in speech, thought, or action in the past? [Insert resounding 'hell no' here]. This is the same man who made the 'Hymie-town' remark during a time when he himself was actively campaigning for President. The same man who carried on an extramarital affair while at the same time serving as 'spiritual counselor' to President Clinton during the Monica Lewinski debacle. The same man who once said he was 'sick and tired of hearing about the Holocaust'. Geesh - Jesse Jackson is a member of the foot-in-mouth Hall of Fame.

Don't get me wrong, peeps. Jesse Jackson has also done plenty of good work, and has been a tireless stalwart for the black community since the days of the Civil Rights Movement, though it's been hard to miss the fact that some of his actions over the last several years have seemed more like opportunities to increase his personal visibility and net worth than genuine attempts at working to change the black condition in this country.

That's what's so dangerous about his careless remarks - when a man who in almost all other ways, claims to have the best interests of the down-trodden minorities in this country at heart, goes and spouts off at the mouth about anything anytime he wants, it lends credence to the idea that many have that he's really only ever trying to draw more attention to himself. And in taking his little jab at the Senator, he unknowingly crossed the line from plain old diarrhea of the mouth, to committing what in my mind will go down in history as one of the classic goofs of all time.

See, what-had-happened-was, after Jesse made his little remark, the Obama Campaign disclosed that the Reverend's very own son, Jesse Jackson Jr., had actually advised the Senator (in part) on what his official response to the Jena 6 case and the trial should be (no - you understood correctly, but go back and read it again if you need to). Yes! It's true! Our friend Reverend Jackson:

- Inserted himself into the limelight surrounding the Jena 6 case, once again squeezing out a spot in the national spotlight for himself while...
- The Obama Campaign looked to the Jr. Jesse Jackson to help Senator Obama craft an official stance on the Jena 6 case, just in time for...
- Big Daddy Jackson to carelessly tell a reporter that in delivering the very same response that his son helped come up with, Senator Obama was 'acting too white'.

Too funny. So in essence, Jesse Jackson Sr. thinks Jesse Jackson Jr. acts too white, and what we really have here is a private family matter between a father disillusioned by his son's sense of his own racial identity, and a son who clearly doesn't call his Dad on the weekends to tell him how he spends his work week.

My suggestion to Mr. Jackson is that he lay down his weapon (his big mouth), take a deep breath, and figure out how he can keep from destroying any legacy he might have left from his involvement in the Civil Rights Movement. He would do well to start by not attacking the one man who in all his actions and deeds has proven that he has the best interest of all people at heart, especially African Americans and those who are disenfranchised, or have been forgotten by modern day politicians and their heartless brand of politics. He would do well to end by somehow choking back the urge now and forever more to belittle anyone's actions by saying they're acting 'too white'. What the hell does that mean, anyway?

Finally, my fervent wish for Jesse Jackson is that he find a clue at the end of one of his rainbows and drag his politically, socially dated butt into the new millennium and find a way to help deal with this nation's problems in the context of the new realities in which we find ourselves - one where people no longer refer to others as 'too black' or 'too white', and one where a black man can really become President of these United States, and is not relegated to just running on a national platform aimed at bolstering his street cred and eliciting the blind faith of black men, women and children in communities nationwide who deserve better. I'm just sayin'.

I Want Hourly Updates

The purpose of erecting the website for Black Women for Obama was to bring important issues to the fore; I knew from the onset that those issues would not always relate directly to the election season, and today's message to you, Dear Readers, has nothing whatsoever to do with the Election of '08. Here goes.

 Over the weekend, Chicago's local media began issuing reports regarding a missing young woman by the name of Nailah Franklin. Nailah is a 28-year old drug sales representative from Chicago who was reported missing after sending a vague text message to friends and family. She had apparently been receiving threatening phone calls from someone she used to date before she disappeared. Nailah Franklin, as you can see from the photo above, is a young black woman.

 So I'm sitting in front of my television as I watch the coverage just shaking my head, because I know that like so many other stories involving missing black women, the public outcry for her safe return will never come; the vigils outside her mother's home, the tearful interviews on Good Morning America begging for any news on her whereabouts - will not happen. And it just pisses me off beyond belief.

I have always been bothered by the way the American media obsesses over non-minority women when they go missing. It says something really disturbing about our society that we put less value on a human life if that life is not wrapped in a package that we think is befitting. I'm bothered because I'm certain that beautiful, intelligent black women are abducted all the time unfortunately, and yet we rarely if ever hear about their stories, except as some passing news item on the network and cable news channels. And maybe even some not-so-beautiful, not-so-educated black women have been lost to their families and loved ones as well - God help them if they live in an inner city. But let a blonde-haired, blue-eyed Caucasian college student come up missing, and the "cable news earth" stops revolving. Major news events are preempted to get the word out, people appear out of nowhere to assist the family and help garner support from their communities, money for rewards start flowing like a river - it's amazing!

I want HOURLY updates on the Nailah Franklin case - I want consistent coverage on the progress of the search for her and I want it to go on forever or until she's found, whichever comes first. In other words, I want her to get the same chance at the oh-so important exposure from the news media that any Natalee Holloway look-a-like would receive. In a nation that prides itself on its multi-culturalism, and that wants to believe it has left the specter of racism behind, why is it seemingly impossible for the media to give fair and equitable coverage to the missing/exploited minorities in this country?

As a professional black woman, with a family who loves me, and with a gaggle of female nieces, young cousins, and friends that I cherish dearly, it pains me to know that if one of them were suddenly gone without a trace, the only hope my family would have of garnering any attention to their story would be a blurb on the local news channel for a night. Meanwhile, the young, white, and attractive that disappear (no matter what the circumstances) end up captivating the ENTIRE world for months and sometimes years on end. Where is the equity in that?

I can ask this question because it's obvious that the spectacle that some of these stories become is COMPLETELY media-driven. We live in a society where we are conditioned to care about, talk about, and believe in whatever the media sends our way. As a sad result, the message that our society is being force-fed is that the value of a black woman's life, or the value of a Latino woman's life is not as important as that of an Anglo-Saxon, and their subsequent abduction or murder is hardly worth reporting.

Of course, it doesn't end there. Missing or abducted younger women are more often reported on than are older women, and most certainly, the more attractive the woman the more coverage she gets.

This is irresponsible on so many levels. How are we as a society going to let the legions of young Black and Hispanic women and girls in this country know that we value them, and that their existence means anything to the future of this nation if we allow such a glaring disparity to continue? I am a college instructor, technology professional, author, mother, daughter and friend to many people who love me dearly. It is so disheartening to know that if I were to ever disappear, the exact same effort that is expended to find young, attractive, white women would not be expended to locate my big, black butt and bring me back to my loved ones.

Remember Latoyia Figueroa? Latoyia was a beautiful young woman who like Nailah was of African-American descent. Latoyia disappeared on July 18, 2005. She was five months pregnant at the time, and was reported missing after she failed to show up to work. At the time, her disappearance did spark some controversy, because all of the major news outlets completely ignored her story, despite the obvious similarities to the Laci Petersen case, and because of their unending fascination with the hot case of the time, Natalee Holloway. However, the controversy was short-lived, and as far as I can tell, no media outlet has been brave enough to lead the charge towards change since. We've successfully integrated the work place, schools, and public restrooms - what's the deal with media coverage?

As a point of illustration, try this. Go to Google (or any other search engine) and search on "Latoyia Figueroa". You should get somewhere in the area of 22,000 hits. Now - type in "Natalie Holloway" (an intentional misspelling of her name) and search. You get more than double the hits, about 47,000, even with her name misspelled! Finally, type in "Natalee Holloway", and do a search. You'll find well over six-hundred THOUSAND references to her, many of them media references, or sites and blurbs that are a direct result of the mountainous amount of coverage her case has received. The inequality is appalling, shocking really, and I submit that it must change before this country can ever really consider itself racially progressive.

I should state emphatically that it is a tragedy whenever *anyone* is abducted - black, white, green, or fuchsia. But it is equally tragic when a nation like this one so openly devalues one segment of its population so blatantly. I plan to watch the coverage of this story VERY closely, and hold the media accountable for not giving this young woman the same chance to be found, and for not giving her family the same chance at closure that Natalee Holloway's and Laci Petersen's families got. It's only fair, and if the media can't be fair about something like this, then hell, what *can* they be fair about?

In Defense of Bill O'Reilly

It's hard being a seeker of truth. Sometimes, when you go looking for it, you're not comfortable with what you find.

It was an email that I received from a colleague that alerted me to the latest Bill O'Reilly flap. When I read its contents, I was of course incensed. It was Friday, and I was preparing for a trip to South Carolina to canvass for the Obama Campaign. On early Saturday morning, two of the members of the Georgia chapter of BWFO here in Georgia and I boarded a van headed for Columbia, South Carolina.

When we arrived, we met other Obama volunteers at the Columbia field office of Obama for America. After a hard day of walking the streets, passing out campaign materials and talking to registered voters, we spent a happy evening having dinner together at the home of the SC State Chapter Director of BWFO, Yvonne Robinson.

At Yvonne's insistence, I was seated at the head of a beautifully decorated table in her formal dining room with several other Obama supporters, who all just happened to be black. This is note-worthy because there were over 60 people in attendance, and an equal number of blacks and whites, though there were a few Asians and Hispanics there as well.

The dinner chat inevitably turned to the remarks Bill O'Reilly had made about Sylvia's Restaurant in Harlem during a conversation with NPR Senior Correspondent Juan Williams on his nationally syndicated radio show. Of course, being the opinionated chick that I am, I happily joined in the castigation:

"I can't believe Bill O'Reilly would say such a thing and think he could get away with it", said one dinner guest.

"What do you expect - we're talking about Bill O'Reilly here. He put the 'R' in racist", said another.

"Oh, you better believe I'm going to get him in my next blog article!" I chimed in gleefully.

And so it went for the rest of the evening. Here and there, people remarking on the irresponsible, blatantly racist comments made by a man who under almost any other circumstance, I would have choked on my own vomit rather than defend. Hmmm. Not the best visual. Sorry.

So we arrive back in Atlanta later that evening, and I drag myself home and fall into bed (walking the streets of Columbia had taken a toll on me). It was the next afternoon before I was rested enough to do a little research so that I could write my scathing rebuke of Bill O'Reilly. I was tingly with anticipation - not since I'd skewered Oprah Winfrey regarding her "I just stopped going" remark had I been so excited about writing a piece.

I read what others had to say about the controversy, in particular the Media Research Council, who are none too happy with Mr. Bill. Then, I ventured onto Bill O'Reilly's website at http://www.billoreilly.com to listen to the re-play of the interview in question in its entirety. I was sure by listening to the full segment myself, I would be able to uncover even more nuggets of on-air joy to slam Bill with.

What I found instead stopped me dead in my tracks.

The segment opened with Bill doing a diatribe about prejudice in America, one that appeared to have been brought on by the question of whether or not blacks would rebel if OJ Simpson were convicted of the charges stemming from the alleged robbery in Las Vegas. Bill gave what could arguably be considered a thought-provoking analysis of why some blacks inevitably defend other blacks, no matter what the evidence or circumstances. The theory he offered was not an inaccurate one - he said basically that blacks in this country have been so discriminated against and so put upon, that now there are two kinds of us - those who have managed somehow to make the conscious decision not to let a history of ongoing wrongs by a racist society cloud our judgment, and those who just can't seem to help themselves, a sentiment with which I just can't disagree.

It was near the beginning of this commentary that he mentioned the trip to Sylvia's and his dinner with Al Sharpton; and yes, he did in fact remark on how surprised he was that the restaurant was like so many others he had visited in New York, but it ended there until a bit later in the show, and that is where those who would hang Bill out to dry have gotten it wrong.

You see, sometime after making that remark, he introduced Juan Williams, and they began a spirited conversation about race relations in America that included a short discussion of the impact of gangster rap on our collective culture. Bill actually defended African Americans, saying that he didn't believe that most blacks love gangster rap (I for one, do not), and he defended us further by remarking that he believes that most black people, like white people, are middle of the road when it comes to the extremes of racism, and the moral carnage of some rap music, with its sexist, demeaning lyrics and glorification of violence. Again, not far off base.

Then it happened - the moment that I believe started all of this. His voice raised in excitement, and playing off of the verbal jabs coming from Juan Williams, Bill made the following remark:

"That's right, that's right - [and] there wasn't one person in Sylvia's screaming M-f-fer, I want more ice-tea!"

I was stunned. I realized immediately that not only had Bill O'Reilly not made a racist comment, but that what he had actually tried to do was use his trip to Sylvia's to illustrate how the media's distortion of blacks could influence what some whites might have expected to find in an all-black restaurant. There was no denying it - O'Reilly had actually made the remark in response to the assertion that white America's view of African Americans has essentially been reduced to the predominant images of blacks in the media - rap videos, perp walks, and a ridiculous spate of reality shows on the par of 'Flavor of Love' and 'Hot Ghetto Mess'. To re-state - Bill O'Reilly was essentially saying that much of White America has been conditioned to believe that all black people are like what they see in rap videos and on reality shows. He was trying to say that nothing could be further from the truth, as evidenced by the fact that during his time at Sylvia's, there wasn't a single person behaving like what we see so often on TV.

I believe in my heart that Bill O'Reilly was trying to engage in a responsible discourse about the state of race relations in America by saying what he did, and that those who naturally want to believe differently, pulled out the salacious parts of his dialog, and strung them together and reported on them in a way that would achieve maximum impact. The conversation was an uncomfortable one to listen to, to be sure - it's always difficult when White America insists on telling us why we are the way we are. But I had to admit to myself that heard in the full context of the discussion, there wasn't a single racist thing about what Bill O'Reilly said, and armed with that knowledge, I had no choice but to defend the man and set the record straight.

So here I am, typing away, feeling robbed, and pondering why this happened, though I think it's as simple as this - we're living in the post-Imus era. There are a select number of television and radio personalities out there that have had targets on their backs (some deservedly so) ever since Don Imus proved in his infinite stupidity that justice can in fact be brought to bear on an irresponsible radio talk show host. And if you're a black woman, you were forced to endure the discomfort of the whole Imus episode, and no doubt are a bit more sensitive of the remarks that some of these guys make then you might have been before - guys like Sean Hannity, Neal Boortz, Rush Limbaugh, and yes, Bill O'Reilly. I don't think any of us could be blamed for a rush to judgment of Mr. O'Reilly without knowing all the facts.

But at least in the case of this latest flap, I'm convinced that lots of people have it wrong, and since I'm convinced of this, it is my duty as a seeker of the truth to stand up and say as much. In a fair and progressive society, it is as important for the socially responsible to stand up and admit when we're wrong, as it is for us to demand justice when we are right. And this time, the people who went after Bill O'Reilly were just plain wrong.

I listen to and watch both Bill O'Reilly and Rush Limbaugh whenever I have the opportunity; people often ask me why. The truth of the matter is I really do seek the truth in all things, not just in what feels comfortable. I personally need to know why there are so many people out there who seem incapable of understanding that this nation has real problems, that there are people who really can't just 'help themselves', and that even with the amazing gains that Blacks in this country have made, there are still those who are caught in a cycle of poverty and hopelessness that can be directly attributed to the lingering effects of slavery. What I've discovered in listening to people like O'Reilly and Limbaugh is that their fervent belief in what they espouse is a direct a result of a number of things - 1) their deeply engrained perspectives on the world, 2) their upbringing, combined with their life experiences and yes, 3) their attitudes towards blacks that have in part been shaped by the images that we've allowed the media and the entertainment industry to propagate over the years.

We have to bear some of the blame. Since becoming a mother and responsible adult, I cringe at the sight of shows like 'Flavor of Love'; I flinch when I see a beautiful young black sister, barely dressed, and draped all over a foul-mouthed rapper; and I even seethe a bit at the thought of some black comedians, who at times can't seem to deliver a single decent joke without using several dozen profane words, only to descend into the same old sexual blathering we've heard a million times over. There's at least one unavoidable truth in what Mr. O'Reilly had to say that day on his radio show, that I fear many black people simply don't want to hear - that by allowing ourselves to be caricaturized in the media by music videos, reality shows and the like, we're helping to add to the belief that we're not much more than what the media insists on portraying us as. This is not to say that the media has not had a heavy hand in crafting our public image; as someone pointed out in response to my recent article on the disappearance of Nailah Franklin, the media wants to sell airtime - that's it. As long as the media believes that people prefer to see blacks being handcuffed and led out of inner-city drug houses, or cat-fighting each other over a man who is truly the ugliest human being alive, that's the kind of fare they'll crank out, and nothing will change. But black people - if they feed it to us, and we consume it, we can't complain when others consume it as well. Period.

Bill O'Reilly has not won a new fan. I've seen too many of his rants and way too many examples of how he's gotten it so very wrong, the Ludacris debacle being the most glaring example. He doesn't understand our culture, and he never will. He chooses to jump all over black rappers when there are white actors and rock stars doing drugs, demeaning women, and getting locked up as well. He clearly has it out for the rap industry, and to me that makes him prejudiced. But his tendency towards snap judgments just means we have to be very careful to choose our battles carefully, and fairly. Rail-roading someone into a bogus controversy without knowing and acknowledging all the facts will do nothing to change things, and I fear, could actually make things worse. I hope by standing up and saying that what's happening right now to Bill O'Reilly is wrong, it will help us cut through the clutter so that we can focus on those times when going after him is the right thing to do.

But I'm sorry. This ain't it.

The Plague of "Single Issue Syndrome"

Now that I've committed myself to supporting the Obama '08 campaign, I find myself involved in discussions around his viability as a candidate, and about the state of politics in the nation as a whole almost on a daily basis.

I talk to friends, strangers, and occasionally a relative or two. In a discussion with one of my closest relatives the other day, we broached the subject of how she will go about making a choice of who she'll support. I of course, was extolling the virtues of Senator Obama, and urging her to learn more about him. She was hesitant, she said for a very good reason.

According to this relative, most people have a single issue that polarizes them, and compels them to throw their support behind one candidate or another; for my niece, that issue is abortion. I can imagine that for many these days, the war in Iraq is a hot-button issue, and for me, the quality of education in this country is a biggie, because I'm of the opinion that if we don't improve the system somehow, we'll find ourselves in a position of diminished competiveness, especially in the fields of technology and science, where we're already reduced to importing young up-starts from Asia and massive outsourcing to stay in the game. Everyone has a single issue which they feel passionately about, and I guess I'm no different.

But my conversation with this particular relative got me thinking - they always do, in fact, because she happens to be a staunch Republican, and was a solid Bush supporter. I say was, because as with most of his fan base, he's lost his shine with her. Which gets me to my point.

I can recall vividly the heated debates she and I had about the potential for a Bush second term. It was during a time when I was convinced that John Kerry would be the next President because as a nation, we were right smack in the middle of the discovery that (oops) there really *were* no weapons of mass destruction in Iraq to speak of and, (double oops), there was no detectable connection between 9/11 and Saddam Hussein. And of course Osama bin Laden was and still is on the loose.

But my niece was adamant that Bush was the right candidate at the time; she, like many Americans at that point were in my opinion completely blinded by Bush's strategy of pandering to the religious right with weak declarations of his belief in God, and his adamant stance against abortion. I got that. But even then, I couldn't help but think to myself the question that many had asked before me - *how can you possibly celebrate this man as a champion and protector of the unborn, knowing that he is directly responsible for the loss of the lives of so many innocent women and children in Iraq, not to mention the loss of so very many of our young soldiers?*

I would submit that the people who supported Bush back then, especially in his second run were inflicted with S.I.S. - *Single Issue Syndrome*, and it IS a syndrome, because the enormity of the job of President of the United States should and could never be reduced to one man's stance on a single issue. As our friend Mr. Bush has demonstrated, even a half-assed attempt at what he called 'compassionate conservatism' in the form of initiatives like *No Child Left Behind* proved to be less than effective at best, and a complete failure at worst. By the time we got to the 2004 election, the totality of who the man was as a president was evident, glaringly so, and yet he pulled the proverbial election rug right out from under John Kerry by tearfully renewing his commitment to God and faith before the nation again and again. And it worked. Yikes.

Please don't get me wrong. I have a strong faith in God, and always have. I was raised to fear and believe in God, and I am raising my son the same way. But the principles upon which this nation were founded should cause us to reject the idea that the way a single man believes religiously should form the basis of whether or not he should or shouldn't be the leader of this great nation. It flies in the face of everything this nation was meant to be, and clouds our vision to the realities of the really tough issues we face.

And so in the last election, we put a man back in office who would keep us on a path in Iraq that even his staunchest supporters now agree was a mistake, and in doing so completely obliterate any of the good will that may have remained between us and other nations around the world (just ask Tony Blair). And why? Because his vision for our nation's future was so compelling? Because he had a solid plan for healthcare reform, our education system, and was well on his way to eliminating our trade deficits and balancing the budget? Nope. We did it because at the end of too many of his rambling speeches, he offered the obligatory 'God bless America'.

I exaggerate of course, but you get my point. For the last couple of decades, we have been headed down a treacherous path, one where real political issues have given way to media coverage that distracts instead of educates, and where politicians have to become so consumed with fund raising and cow-towing to special interests that the noise level is just deafening. And nothing gets done. And the major issues that plague us grow worse and worse. I have decided this time that I will not support anyone who doesn't have a real vision for our nation as a whole. Senator Obama has convinced me that not only does he *have* that vision, but it's a fair and balanced one (to use the phrase of a popular news network) one in which he will position himself to work with both sides of the political aisle to tackle the tough issues we face - our dependence on foreign oil, our broken healthcare and education systems, and of course the mess that is the war in Iraq.

His vision is inclusive of everyone in the nation, and *that's* why he's where he is today, having raised more money this last quarter than any Presidential candidate in history; his message is resounding with the American people, people from every race, age group and from every walk of life. I have committed myself to helping spread that message because I believe in it. All of it.

I encourage you to look at the man for yourself. Read *The Audacity of Hope* and the many speeches and other information we've compiled on BWFO.org. We can't afford to suffer collectively from S.I.S., not this time, there's too much at stake. Only when we're able to look at the issues we face as a complete and complex whole, can we make the right decisions about who can most effectively lead us out of the darkness of the past few administrations to a brighter, more prosperous future.

Clarence Thomas versus Anita Hill: 16 Years Later

I was still a young woman when Anita Hill was forced to make public her accusations that Justice Clarence Thomas had sexually harassed her while she was in his employ at the US Department of Education and later at the EEOC.

It was 1991. I was 25 years old, still pondering what I would ultimately do with my life (sadly), and barely getting by. As a matter of fact, during those now infamous confirmation hearings, I was unemployed, after having just moved to the Atlanta area with my new husband, and I dare say, I spent more time riveted to the television set watching the drama of those hearings unfold than I should admit.

Clarence Thomas was almost assured of winning the nomination that would make him only the second African-American to ever serve on the Supreme Court when a leaked FBI report caused the Judiciary

Committee to delay a final vote on his confirmation in order to get to the bottom of the allegations that had been reported. What ensued was days of smarmy testimony from Justice Thomas and Anita Hill that at once captivate and divided the nation, with its graphic details of remarks allegedly made by Justice Thomas. Ultimately of course, Thomas was confirmed by a historically narrow margin, and Ms. Hill's brave appearance before the Judiciary Committee faded into history.

I can remember feeling a distinct sense of shame back then over watching two otherwise prominent black professionals air their laundry in front of that congressional panel, none of whom were black, and none of whom were women. It just didn't seem right, though it was certainly historic on many fronts. The Clarence Thomas-Anita Hill saga brought the issue of sexual harassment to the forefront of the national consciousness with a vengeance -I'm certain that no professional male since has been quite as careless in their remarks to a female subordinate.

This week, Justice Clarence Thomas released a new book, entitled "My Grandfather's Son", in which he recounts his life and the events of the 103 days leading up to his Supreme Court confirmation. He also uses the work to continue to besmirch the character of Anita Hill, which is a real shame. With the release of Justice Thomas' book, Ms. Hill (now a professor of Policy and Law at Brandeis University) has had to yet again go on the defensive after all these years. Way back then, most Americans watched the proceedings, and decided that she was some sort of paid Democratic operative, or even worse - a desperate, confused liar. That's most Americans. But not me.

I can distinctly remember asking myself even then, "Why would a woman, *any* woman, subject herself to such unyielding personal scrutiny, such outright attacks, just to gain notoriety or financial gain?" It just didn't add up. Those who labeled Anita Hill a liar insisted that her continued professional relationship with Clarence Thomas was evidence that she clearly had not been harassed. Further, Justice Thomas himself went to great pains to paint her as a neurotic woman, who was mediocre in her work performance and prone to mental instability, though he has somehow gotten away with never explaining why he hired her not once, but twice to work for him.

For me, it boils down to this:

Anita Hill was approached by the FBI during the confirmation hearings after *they* learned that she had mentioned allegations of impropriety on the part of Justice Thomas to a colleague. She did not seek them out. She was approached about those conversations, and consented to recount them on the record *only* under the condition that the information never become public knowledge. This fact is a matter of public record. With that being the case, it perplexes me that anyone would think that she set out to smear the man.

Again - the Senate Judiciary Committee was at the point of sending Justice Thomas' nomination to the Senate for final confirmation when a pair of journalists found out about Ms. Hill's secret testimony and leaked the information to the news media. There were plenty of accusations leveled, and much speculation about who actually leaked the information - whether it was a Democratic hatchet job, or some other blatant attempt to derail the Justice's nomination, but the fact that there might have been an ulterior motive on the part of the leaker, didn't change the fact that Anita Hill was a reluctant participant. Much later in the proceedings, when it was much too late to matter, at least one other woman came forward and admitted that she had endured the same kind of unprofessional behavior at the hands of Justice Thomas.

Further, Clarence Thomas' defense of himself never rang true to me, not then and not now. In remarks he delivered to the Judiciary Committee, he denied ever attempting to have anything more than a cordial, platonic relationship with Anita Hill, and claimed to have "wracked his brain" trying to think of what he could have said that would have caused Ms. Hill to make such charges. There was just way too much righteous indignation in his testimony. A "high-tech lynching?" To compare what he endured at the hands of the Judiciary Committee to the misery that black men who were literally lynched suffered at the hands of the evil, murderous racists in this country made me nauseous, and was remarkably self-serving. He played the ultimate race card, in a situation where there was no evidence of racial bias. Maybe political bias, but not racial.

The other striking thing for me was the detailed way in which Ms. Hill described the interactions between her and Justice Thomas. It was chilling, and just way too weird to be fabricated. I mean, she could have gone for the typical, "he grabbed my ass", or, "he threatened to fire me if I didn't sleep with him", but the stories she recounted sounded much more like a long-term professional relationship that at least one party thought was familiar enough that they could say pretty much anything they wanted - for laughs, for shock value, for whatever reason. Pubic hairs on Coke cans? Who would make something like *that* up as an accusation? It just doesn't make sense.

Then, there's Anita Hill herself. A professional law graduate, anxious to make her mark in the legal field - she must have gotten pretty tired of hearing it. "Well, if that all *really* happened, then why did you stay?", and, "No way that happened - wouldn't someone else have come forward?", or my favorite, "She was paid off by the Democratic Party to ruin the man's life - she should be *ashamed* of herself!"

I can remember thinking to myself then, and I'm even surer now that there is an easy explanation for it all, an explanation that in today's social and political climate makes all the sense in the world. Here's my theory.

Back in 1991, there was no Oprah Winfrey to stamp a collective national persona on the black woman. There was no Carol Moseley Braun, no Mae Jemison (she would fly her only shuttle mission a year later), heck, there wasn't even a Cynthia McKinney to give relevance to the political and professional might of black women back then. Anita Hill was a national anomaly, and I would submit, a sad victim of a society that just plain didn't know what to do with a black female making such accusations. It was much easier for most people to believe that she was some kind of rare nutcase than it was to believe that Clarence Thomas was a typical, dare I say it, black man, prone to bouts of lewdness and off-color commentary in a close-knit work environment. Since that time, I've seen it myself - not so much from a subordinate's point of view, but I know how black men and women can get within the confines of a closed space when they think they can't be heard.

And that's the tough part for me, because I really have always felt that what we all witnessed way back then was a dynamic that occurs all too often between black men and women, being held up to a standard that most other cultures wouldn't understand. I don't believe that Justice Thomas *thought he was harassing* Anita Hill, any more than I believe that Anita Hill meant to use the information she shared with some colleague in confidence to completely trash her good name trying to go after Justice Thomas. Things took place. Planets aligned. And then it all took on a life of its own.

And though it brought an important issue to the nation's attention, the unfair light that was cast on Anita Hill was a blow to black women, plain and simple. She should be regarded as a hero for being brave enough to tell her story under such hostile circumstances; instead, she will forever be known by most as the accuser of a 'great' man, hell bent on sabotaging the confirmation of a man who was trying to make history by becoming only the second African American Supreme Court Justice. Those of us who believed her then and believe her now know that nothing could be farther from the truth, and that in standing her ground back then, she made a mark that in some ways was just as important as Justice Thomas'. One in which a black woman, standing alone and wrongly vilified stood up for what's right no matter what the personal cost to her.

Mosquito Diplomacy

Sometimes the nightly political news, chocked full of the sound-bite jabs candidates take at one another is just comical. Sometimes it's even thought-provoking, and at other times it's downright scary. At times of course, it's all three.

Recently, every Democrat in the 2008 Presidential race came out swinging at Senator Obama when during a press conference where he gave a major foreign policy talk, an AP reporter asked whether or not he would use nuclear weapons to 'defeat terrorism' and to 'kill Osama Bin Laden'. No - no, stop laughing. That was really the question. The following was his response:

"I think it would be a profound mistake for us to use nuclear weapons in any circumstance, involving civilians...Let me scratch that. There's been no discussion of nuclear weapons. That's not on the table."

(Source: Cnn.com)

(Hmmm...Divide the first number, carry the one, multiply the mean by the deviated co-efficient) Nope - still sounds reasonable to me.

Now, I'm not normally paranoid, nor do I consider myself to be a conspiracy theorist; I also try my darndest to never be rude, but unfortunately this evening as my gorgeous son reads every word I type aloud, and nuzzles my arm impatiently, waiting for me to just stop working, I fear I'm going to have to be all three.

Is it me, or are a group of our fine Democratic friends a little too gleeful about what they are of course now trying to portray as a political misfire by our favorite Senator? I've haven't seen a group of people this happy about the words coming out of someone's mouth since I announced to my students that class was cancelled a few weeks back. From the Divine Ms. Hillary, to Governor Bill ("I love ya all as my Veep") Richardson, they all had something to say about what I consider to be an intensely loaded question, one that I dare say I've never heard any of the other candidates OR President Bush have to answer. I'm just saying.

But listen, folks. Even *I* am not paranoid enough (yet) to suggest that the AP reporter with his out of the blue, hyper-hypothetical, would-you-risk-unleashing-Armageddon-on-an-entire-nation-of-women-and-children-just-to-toast-one man question was somehow planted in the audience at the press conference by the

Dems or anyone else; but one has to wonder, doesn't
one?

As for the nuclear question itself, I mean, gee. I watch a
lot of news coverage, and like many who oppose the war
in Iraq, I've often wondered to myself why it is exactly
that we *have* to fight the war on terror either in *Iraq* or
here on our shores; I mean to say, I've watched
President Bush repeatedly mutter the same phrase over
and over again when pressed to justify why we're still in
Iraq, spending colossal amounts of money each day that
could be used to rid our country of important things like
illit-, uh, elitt, uh, people who can't read or spell:

*"Our immediate strategy is to eliminate terrorist threats
abroad so we do not have to face them here at home."*

(Source: Every Speech George Bush Has Made In The
Last Four Years)

Ah - that's right - got it. The thing is though, *abroad* is a
pretty, well, broad term. Couldn't abroad mean
Pakistan, where they pretend to be our friends but
yet seem to have a gift for hiding their "You Too Can Be
A Nut-Job Terrorist" training camps? Or couldn't abroad
mean Afghanistan, where, after all, it's generally
believed that Osama bin Laden was last detected by
American intelligence? Why, my dear friends, are we
NOT fighting the war on terrorism in earnest in Pakistan
and Afghanistan, instead of pummeling Iraq, a people
and a country, who though very grateful to be free

of Saddam Hussein's dictatorial regime, also have been, let's just say 'less than shy' about their desire to see us get out of their affairs and go on to the next botched war? And lastly, why (oh friggin', why) hasn't someone asked Bush (gee, I dunno) "Hey! Got any plans to actually *secure* the borders, or to get our brave soldiers out of that country that never ever really posed an imminent threat to us in the first place, in favor of going after the weird lookin' bearded dude that mocked us on video after killing over three-thousand of our citizens? Oh - and will you be using a nuclear weapon to do so?!?"

This brings us to the downright scary. Isn't threatening to 'win the war on terrorism' or 'kill Osama bin Laden with a nuclear weapon' like threatening to get a mosquito out of your car with a wrecking ball? I mean to the normal and reasonable among us, doesn't the very notion of annihilating an entire country just to get one man sound kind of, I dunno - creepy?

Which brings me back to my original point, if in fact I had one. To go all political on Senator Obama over a question that strains credulity is a waste of political brain power, and I'm surprised the candidates don't see it that way. I would love for the AP to hunt them all down one by one, hog tie them and throw them down in front of a few dozen hot lights and a camera, and force them all to answer the same question. I dare say none of them could come up with a rational answer to such an irrational question.

Bottom line? There was nothing in Senator Obama's remarks that said inexperience or lack of judgment to me, though that's exactly what the feigned outrage from his Democratic opponents is meant to convey. All I heard in his response was the honest reaction of a man whose foresight in 2002 proved he is the sole voice of reason among this year's Democratic field of contenders. Senator Obama has shown us yet again that he is a man of principle, who would think first of the good of mankind, and not go to the ugliest of extremes in answering a dopey question, not even if it means looking like less than a tough guy to impress a bunch of reporters anxious to capture any misstep on tape so that they can blast it into 'YouTube land' for all eternity.

I say, "Bravo, Senator Obama". You'd rather try every other option (including waging war in the right countries) before you'd drop an ending-life-as-we-know-it bomb on a population of innocent women and children, huh? Wow, I wish you'd made your voice heard before we got ourselves into this mess in Iraq - oh wait, you did...

From Aristocracy to Democracy: Not in My America

Earlier this year in one of my very first blog entries, I asked the question "Did you know that there has been either a Clinton or a Bush in the White House for almost twenty years?" Back then, I forgot to mention that if you include George H.W. Bush's time as Vice President, you have to pile eight more years on to that number:

President George HW Bush 1980-1991 (as VP and President)

President Bill Clinton 1992-1999

President George W Bush 2000-2007

Almost twenty-eight years of Clintons and Bush's in the White House? What the hell is going on, and what the hell are we in for next?:

President Hillary Clinton 2008- 2015 **(over my dead, maggot infested body)**

President Jeb Bush 2016-2023

President Chelsea Clinton 2024-2031

President Jenna Bush....and on and on and on?

I mean for real - am I the only one that's bothered by the fact that our nation seems in danger of being hijacked by a political aristocracy?

Dwell on that for a moment while you read the definition of "aristocracy", courtesy of *Dictionary.com:*

ar·is·toc·ra·cy

–noun, plural -cies.

1. a class of persons holding exceptional rank and privileges, esp. the **hereditary nobility**.

2. a government or state ruled by an aristocracy, **elite, or privileged upper class**.

3. government by those considered to be the best or **most able people in the state.**

4. a governing body composed of those considered

to be the **best or most able people in the state**.

5. any class or group considered to be superior, as
    through **education, ability, wealth, or social
    prestige**.

(Clearing my throat, cracking my knuckles, and
adjusting myself in my seat.)

At no time in the history of this nation have two families
had such a death grip on the highest office in the land.
It's an odd development in a country that prides itself on
expanding opportunity to anyone who works hard
enough, plays by the rules, and has what it takes to make
it. Suddenly, that all applies to pretty much every job in
our society except the one where it should apply the
most - the Presidency of the United States.

Have we really descended into such mediocrity as a
nation that only a few "able" families, superior in stature
by nature of their education, ability, wealth, social
prestige and noble heritage are qualified to govern us? Is
the prospect of a President David I. Smith (my gorgeous
son) just completely out of the question now, and if so,
why?

I have a very close friend who I love to argue with about
the Obama-Clinton rivalry, because he is so adamant that
Hillary deserves his vote, yet he has no idea why. The
best thing he can come up with is that she brings "built in

political power and experience" to the office, and that at a time like this, we need as much political might as we can get.

I laugh at him when he says this. I tell him that the notion that Hillary Clinton would yield any more political power than Senator Obama or any other candidate who might become the next President is ridiculous. I remind him that it has been the case since the beginning of this nation's history that *becoming* Leader of the Free World comes with all the political power anyone could need, whoever that someone is. Then, I lovingly remind him that there is absolutely *no* precedence for what we're witnessing this election year, and that his judgment (like Hillary's during the vote on the Iraq War) is clouded.

Think about it - after having George H.W. Bush do a term as president, a young upstart from Arkansas cleans his clock in his re-election bid, and becomes one of the most popular Presidents in recent memory (even if he was one of the most scandal-laden). After two terms, a rough and tumble Texas Governor by the name of (gasp!) George *W.* Bush is pushed to the national forefront by forces unseen and becomes the *next* President of the United States. Well, all hell breaks loose. The worst attack on our nation's soil since Pearl Harbor results in misstep after misstep from this one - "Mission Accomplished" on the deck of the aircraft carrier USS Abraham Lincoln, then "Oops my bad, still thousands more of our young to sacrifice", and then "It's all Sadaam's fault", and then "Oops, maybe not so much, my bad again", and then finally "We need mo' money, mo' money, mo' money for Iraq, because if we keep throwing money at the problem, we'll eventually win", yada, yada, yada....

Just when we think *this* hell is about to come to an end - *another* blankety-blank Clinton - excuse me - the *wife* no less of the *first* Clinton steps up to remind us that apparently only two families are capable of running the country. Running it into the ground, maybe. What gives?

I'm sure none of us is quite certain of how it happened, but something is definitely amiss. The stranglehold these two families have on American politics is darned un-American, and I would submit highly out of step with what our fore fathers envisioned for our country. I think that if they could, they'd bitch slap each and every American who would dare contemplate voting for Hillary Clinton just because she has some perceived political might that is somehow magically unattainable for anyone whose name is not Bush or Clinton. That's poppy-cock. The notion makes no sense whatsoever.

I think the problem comes down to 1) a real need for campaign finance reform, and 2) the need to kick a lazy American electorate in its collective ass. Hard.

For many reasons - technological advancements, the proliferation of new media and communications, hell, 24-hour news channels - the way to win elections is to bring in the money. Candidates for office in this country are consumed with raising money, because they know that it's the only way to get the massive marketing machine cranked up that they'll need to keep their faces in front of the public. And because it is that marketing machine, with its 15 second sound bites, 30 second tear-jerker campaign ads, and new age substance-less, repetitive debates that drives us politically, he who markets the best wins the races. Poop on what a candidate actually stands for, or what they actually bring to an office - all we care about is how much his friggin' hair cut costs!

Imagine if all Presidential candidates were given a 1 million dollar budget, and weren't allowed to spend another thin dime, how much more substantive their messages would become. How much more knowledgeable of the candidates might *we* become, if we had to seek out their positions, or god-forbid, pick up a book and read all about them? And how *even* would the playing field become if the power-fundraisers with their special interest buddies didn't always lead the pack? See where I'm going with this?

What makes it even worse is the laziness of the American people. We are all now so used to learning about our future leaders in 30 second snippets, through pointless and stilted election ads, and yes, through the oh-so-powerful media, that we no longer even think for ourselves. We don't pull back the layers of any candidate to get to what's real. We rely on what the media feeds us, and what we're most comfortable with believing without actually having to burn off a brain cell to help us choose who we elect to political office, and that's a low down dirty shame.

The Clintons may have some political clout, but is it the kind of clout that brings good judgment and results-driven governance to the White House? When the campaigning is over, and the votes have been tallied, and it's time to bring our troops home, solve our most pressing social problems, and restore our reputation in the world, do we really believe the people that have had their foots on our necks for the last twenty years can bring about that change?!?

Not me. And I can say definitively that I *have* pulled back the layers of the candidates, for the first time in my life, and what I know about them, and what I've learned about Senator Obama has made my choice as clear as day.

Another twenty years of Clintons and Bushes? Only if we've given up on the idea of a real democracy. Only if we've decided to give in to evolving into an aristocracy, and I just can't believe that's the case. We want more for our nation than that, pure and simple. We want the continued ideals of government for the people and by the people, and no one exemplifies those ideals more than Senator Barack Obama. That's why I know that Senator Obama *will* be the next President of the United States, because the American people will not be held hostage by political elitism. Not now, not ever. Not in *my* America.

Commas for Obama #3

If you've read any of the past "Commas for Obama"
posts, you know that the goal here is to seek out
opportunities for dialog for the political edification and
reading pleasure of BWFO readers.

And so today, in a new installment of "Commas for
Obama: We Pause for Thought", we present a response
to a previous blog entry entitled "Democracy to
Aristocracy: Not in My America", written by yours truly,
of course.

If you're a regular reader, you recall that this
article points out the back to back "Bush-Clinton-Bush"
presidencies, and discusses the possibility of (cringe)
another Clinton in the White House in the context of a
new-age aristocracy.

Well - the response to the post was incredible! I received
death threats, anonymous, ominous calls to my home in
the middle of the night, my tires were slashed, my house

was painted with graffiti - okay not really. I did receive several *really* heated responses to my assertion that Americans have collectively rolled over and allowed two families to occupy the highest office in the land for nearly a quarter of a century, though. My favorite is the subject of this edition of CFO, and comes from a woman who identifies herself only as GeorgiaCEOToday.

Original message from GeorgiaCEOToday: --------------

Dear Black Women for Obama:

Patricia, I disagree with you!

There were 65 pages of legal notices from foreclosures last weekend in the AJC. Today, we are on the **verge of a recession** as jobs are outsourced to India, Russia, China or other places that don't respect the same human rights, employment, or product quality standards as we do. The dollar is weak. Greenspan suggests that capital be moved out of industrial jobs (GM) and into cutting edge technology which is a hard hit for America's autoworkers. Instead of feeling sorry for children in Cambodia, you may one day watch as Korea takes pity on our ability to feed American children.

With that, I begin my vehement and angry criticism of your blog *Not in My America.*

While the Hillary supporters, and certainly the Bush supporters sure can be vicious at times, your candidate, Barack Obama seemed a breath of fresh air in Washington's politics as usual.

Why then should Barack Obama supporters like you, stoop to the level of demonstrating the same meanness and triviality that Karl Rove is famous for? If that is what you are doing, I can't be a part of it.

[PAS] Your illustration of the issues that plague our nation is eloquent and thorough, and completely on the mark. Meanness and triviality, though? Comparing me to Karl Rove? That says to me that you completely missed the point of my blog entry.

Was it Rove who came up with the idea that Dukakis was single handedly responsible for releasing hundreds of Black rapists and murderers into the streets of Massachusetts's? Of course it was terrible, but also genius in its ability to play to the fears of millions of **white voters** by equating Dukakis with **Black prisoners**.

So now, Patricia, is it you who will play to the fears of **black women** by equating Hillary with Marie Antoinette, when you state that she is playing "dress up" with the leader of the Republican Party....the same party that attempted to impeach her husband?

[PAS] **Rapists and murderers? That's a pretty dramatic thing to pull out of your hat. The reference to Hillary and George playing dress-up is directly related to the point of the article, and nothing more. To assert that I meant it in any other way is quite frankly ludicrous, and to compare me (again) to Karl Rove as if I am some stealth political operative says to me that you're perspective on things has been clouded by too many years spent in the political fray. It is not my intent in anything that I write to do anything but state my opinion, and in my opinion, the current state that we find ourselves in as a nation is in part due to the way this country has been led over the last several decades, and that includes the Clinton years. I have in no way implied that Hillary is "cozying" up to the Republican Party - you drew that conclusion on your own.**

And even if Hillary Clinton and President Bush are playing dress up or footsie together behind closed doors...is that a strong and sensible reason to vote for Obama? What in the world does that have to do with health care, or the WAR for Goodness Sakes??? People are dying!

Even worse, you ask whether our nation is in jeopardy of being hijacked by a political aristocracy!!!!!! Rule by the aristocracy didn't begin with George H. W. Bush.

Forget that Washington and Jefferson were Vice-President and President 20 years, have you **NOT** noticed

102

in your entire life, or any history books that there have almost always been wealthy or educated families leading our nation (Roosevelt's, Adams, Kennedy's)? Have you not noticed that if they were not wealthy as children, they almost always were legally or militarily trained before becoming President, to better interpret and enforce our nation's laws (Lincoln, Clinton, Eisenhower, Jackson)?

Read the Federalist Papers! Rule by a talented and able few has always been the plan. There was much debate from the founders of the nation as to how to create a nation that was not a kingdom.

Anyway, the word "Aristocracy" comes from Aristotle (see Poetics, Politics). In other words, the aristocracy wasn't invented by George W. Bush but it is a very old idea that those who are best educated and most wise govern the common populace.

[PAS] The problem is not that we are being ruled by wealthy and educated families; the problem is that we have been ruled for almost the last thirty years by the same TWO wealthy and educated families! Do your homework! The foothold these two families has had on the office of the Presidency is UNHEARD OF in HISTORY! The only thing that even comes close is the father-son presidencies of John Adams and John Quincy Adams (24 years apart), and the presidencies of Theodore Roosevelt and Franklin D. Roosevelt (fifth cousins) which were also separated by 25 years!

Also - let's face it - in terms of their political agendas, there is not a whole lot of difference between any of the field of Democratic hopefuls - so in the end, it comes down to who has the best vision for the country, and who has the best record of displaying good judgment in the face of things like 9/11 and the Iraq War. Hillary loses on both points - Senator Obama wins. It also comes down to who can best work to make the changes that you yourself have pointed out are so desperately needed - again, Senator Obama has a proven record of being able to reach across the aisle to work with legislators and get things done. Hillary's most infamous attempt at a national initiative (Healthcare Reform) failed in defeat because of her and Bill Clinton's inability to compromise. This is a matter of record. Look it up.

Also - at no time WHATSOEVER did I say that the aristocracy was created by George W. Bush. Your comments are beginning to border on hysterics - we would have a much more meaningful dialogue about this if you could resist the urge to misinterpret my statements and put words in my mouth!

Still, despite your wonderful imagination, any friendship between Hillary & Bush has nothing to do with **Barack Obama** and really is insulting to all the hard work he has put forth to present Democratic ideas that might help our country through this challenging time. This aristocracy...this democracy, this Republic, you besmirch ....not a dictatorship, not the communist party, not an oligarchy.... allows a talented few, even if poor.... rise up through hard work, education and talent to leadership.

King Louis XIV and Marie Antoinette who you patterned George Bush and Hillary after were not examples of aristocracy.................................... but rather a **MONARCHY.**

While the dictionary provides various connotations of the word Aristocracy, please look at one of the definitions you provided.

4. a governing body composed of those considered to be the **best or most able people in the state**.

Despite that he is not from the Bush or Clinton family, **Mr. Obama**, an attorney of humble beginnings, certainly seems to have grown up to become one of the best and most able. So is **Mr. Edwards,** who wasn't rich, but did gain legal training to govern our society with just laws. So is **Bill Richardson**, another legally trained Democrat who hardly grew up wealthy.

Listen to their ideas!!!!!

Listen to their ideas!!!!!

[PAS] Again - more hysterics. Spreading the word about Senator Obama's ideas are what Black Women

For Obama is and has always been about from the beginning. Your rash judgment of this one blog entry shows beyond a shadow of a doubt that you've not read anything else I've written, which is not a crime, but should be taken into consideration if you're going to cast aspersions on my writing and opinions. And the imagination thing? That's the picture I chose for the article driving you crazy I guess, because I never ONCE mentioned that Hillary and George Bush were friends, or playing "footsie" as you put it. The picture is merely a caricature meant to illustrate the point of the article, which is the danger of our political process being taken over by a new age aristocracy. Again, If you'd seen or read any of my past blogs, you'd likely be a little less distressed over this one.

See why it is that they have risen to leadership from their humble beginnings. Learn what your candidate wants to do. Autoworkers are striking. Soldiers are dying. Cancer victims have no health care. Children are starving in this country. Veterans have to wait to get medical treatment. Katrina victims are still displaced.

Please do not insult all of these issues or me with trivialities!

Tell us something and inspire us why Barack Obama will fix the issues at hand. This election is too important for a Democrat to talk nonsense. Yes, the last one was important but this may be the last opportunity to steer the train away from the cliff.

[PAS] Again - it has practically become my life's work of late to tell people what Senator Obama can and will do to fix the many issues at hand. I've walked the streets of South Carolina in the blinding heat, going from house to house speaking directly with Hillary supporters, Obama supporters, and people who don't know WHO they support to understand their very personal concerns and to talk to them about how Senator Obama will address them. Have you canvassed for Hillary? Made any calls? Even licked a stamp? I HAVE to know everything about Senator Obama's message, because I'm committed like you wouldn't BELIEVE to seeing him get elected. If you're insulted by this blog entry, I encourage you to read some of the others - like "IPods & Sneakers: The Mis-education of Oprah Winfrey". Or, "Jesse Jackson's Jaw Jappin'", or "In Defense of Bill O'Reilly". I will always, ALWAYS tell it like I see it, even if my opinion isn't popular - if you don't agree that is your prerogative. If you're insulted, that's your problem.

There is nothing trivial about my take on the issues, and certainly nothing trivial about the idea that we've become a society of voters that are too lazy to drill down into the issues to understand them, or the candidates. You're fooling yourself if you don't believe that there are lots and lots of people out there

who will cast a vote for Hillary Clinton simply because of her association with her husband - it is THOSE people that BWFO seek out and want to educate. Quite frankly, you are not our target demographic - you're not an Obama supporter, and that's your right, but I've made it my business to find those people who don't know that there is a better alternative out there and educate them. I encourage you to use whatever forum you have at your disposal to do the same, because after all, this is America, and you can do that. In the meantime, please keep reading my blog entries and voicing your opinion. Without this kind of dialog, it's very difficult to get to the truth of a matter, and if YOU jumped to ridiculously erroneous conclusions after reading "Democracy to Aristocracy", others may have as well.

Thanks for helping me set the record straight.

Translating Hype into Votes

I had an interesting conversation with a friend today.

We were discussing Senator Obama's 'hype-factor'; how he seems to have the market cornered on pure [blank] appeal - you can literally plug sex, mass, whip, broad, cross-over, or almost any other kind of appeal into the blank and accurately describe the man.

My friend mentioned that he hoped that Senator Obama could turn the 'hype' into votes. I agreed, of course, but it immediately occurred to me that his statement revealed a series of interesting dilemmas, especially for BWFO.

Dilemma #1 - if you're a single black woman, and you've started or joined an organization called "Black Women for Obama", you are clearly in danger of getting the "Humph - you just like him 'cause he cute" remarks from friends, family, and the occasional total stranger. I'm certain that there is a partial truth in that, I mean, heck, I'm not blind, and as far as I know, neither are any of the current members of BWFO. I see what the man looks like - for the love of Pete, look at ANY picture of him! He is very attractive, there's no doubt about it, so to those people I say - "Duh!"

Yes - it's hard for even a serious (clear throat) writer like me to deny that Senator Obama is a cutie, but the fact is, even a slightly over-sexed, work-a-holic, love-starved, Internet junkie like me can keep my admiration for the Senator at bay, if for no other reason than out of respect for Mrs. Obama...

That was a cry for help if I've ever heard one. Let's move on.

...and because not doing so is darned inappropriate if one expects to be taken seriously.

Dilemma #2 - it's no secret that Senator Obama has a special appeal for the masses. References to the Senator have shown up in rap lyrics, on t-shirts, in music videos, and on college campuses all around the country. People from all walks of life have been mesmerized by his easy-going manner, and ability to connect with a crowd, and most recently he has been described in debate performances as 'genuine', and 'more likable' than the rest of the Democratic field . He oozes likability. The stories of his rock-star receptions at the events he attends are legendary by now. It's an inconvenient truth- the man has star power.

Dilemma #3 - who couldn't help but tear up a bit when they see blacks and whites standing side by side, joyously waving "Obama '08" banners as if their lives depended on it. I'm old enough to remember when a black politician of any kind was a complete novelty, and when the very notion of a black President of the United States was so far-fetched that most people never even discussed the possibility. We are far from completely united in terms of race relations in this country, of course, but the images of Senator Obama being surrounded by people of all kinds, or being happily received by folks in towns both big and small, urban and rural, white and black, give me all of the cause in the world to hope, and inspires more than its share of hype.

So then what *of* the 'hype' factor? If it's hard for me to contain the obvious crush I have on the Senator, is it possible that my friend is right, and that all of the hoopla, all of the media attention, all of the fervor that Senator Obama's campaign has generated *is* just hype?

Nah - here's my take. I also think John Edwards is a cutie. He is - I can admit that. When he does that thing with his hands when he's really trying to make a point - yuuuuum-y. And Rudy Giuliani certainly does have his share of Internet groupies, though I'm guessing a couple of them are probably already in line to be his next ex-wife. And the Hill-ster most definitely does have a broad base of appeal, if not across party lines, certainly across racial ones. She has Billy-boy to thank for that.

111

Then what is it? Why *does* the Senator invoke such a reaction in so many, and how can that reaction be translated into votes?

I'll tell you what, I'll tell you why, and I'll tell you how. Senator Obama helps people like GQ sell magazines not just because he's gorgeous (and he is) - but because *his message excites people.* The idea of a different kind of government doing things a different way just *excites* people. His intelligence, his insightfulness, his wisdom, his sense of family, his diverse background, his humble beginnings, and yes, his mega-watt smile - all combine to create a persona that seems to symbolize everything that America is about.

So how then do we translate all of that into votes? Well, if you're Patricia Wilson-Smith (and I just happen to be), you target the demographic that you are most familiar with, in my case black women, and you vow to do everything in your power to help that demographic see *beyond* the GQ magazine spreads, the 30 second sound bites, and the rap video shout outs to get to why Senator Obama, who *is* intelligent, insightful, wise, and all the rest, is uniquely qualified to lead this nation at a time when:

- the Bush Administration is using every Jedi-mind trick in the book to sell us on the 'successes' in the Iraq War
- the rest of the world thinks we've lost our monkey-a%$# minds

- Our schools are falling into disrepair, and turning out fewer and fewer accomplished students
- Our healthcare system is failing way more of our citizens than it should be and
- the Black family, the stability and viability of our communities, and the very idea of opportunity for the masses is under attack

(Bullet pointed for emphasis, and to prove I'm good at formatting stuff)

In elections, there is no such a thing as over-exposure; getting the image and name of your candidate burned into the very psyches of the American voter is Job 1. So it should come as no surprise to any of us that the Senator would grace the cover of magazines, hang out with Jon Stewart (who wouldn't want to - another yum cake) or crop up as a new icon of the Hip Hop generation. But it's clearly not enough that everyone recognizes him - they have to get off their kiesters on election day and go and cast a vote for him. That's where we at BWFO and Senator Obama's other supporters come in.

Those of us who have committed to working on the Senator's behalf are all busy organizing GOTV events, voter registration drives, house parties, and fund raisers, all designed to disseminate as much real and substantive information about the candidate as possible. We'll let the news media and the national campaign choose his photo-ops; we're working to make sure that everyone we can reach gets to know the Senator's ideas.

And the national campaign is working hard to make sure that ordinary Americans like me all over the country are playing an active role in getting the message out - his is one of the first campaigns ever to make the every-day voter a crucial part of spreading the word, and the only one I've ever known to actively work at building a grass-roots machine that is meant to remain in place long after he's taken up residence in 1600 Pennsylvania Avenue.

And so there is a place in all of this for the 'hype' machine, right along-side the 'truth' machine. We'll use the truth machine to see to it that the realities of the issues plaguing the nation are put in front of American after American, until the day comes when it will be obvious to everyone, even those who know how cute I *really* think Senator Obama is, that it's about so much more than that for me, and his legion of supporters. It's about electing our greatest chance at a unified, transformed-for-the-better America. Period.

A final parting shot - if it was *really* only about cute, heck - Al Sharpton and that fly little comb back? Va-voom!

The "Bill" Factor

There are many reasons why I support Senator Obama, and they are all very well documented on BlackWomenForObama.org. But one of the less talked-about reasons for all my hard work, the thing that drives me to continue to get the word out about the Senator by any means necessary, has to do with the phenomenon that can best be described as "The Bill Factor". Not to be confused with "The Factor" or Fox News or even Bill O'Reilly. Just so you know.

The "Bill Factor" of which I speak of course, is the *Bill Clinton* factor, and the presumption by most that Hillary Clinton has the black vote on lock because of Bill Clinton's popularity as former President. For sure, it would be naive of me to think anything other than that Senator Clinton's name and association to her wildly popular husband makes it very easy to roll over and go to sleep on the rest of the campaign if you're a black voter. No one could blame us at all if we simply chilled until election day and showed up at the polls to pull the lever for the woman who is the wife of the man affectionately known as the "First Black President (FBP)". Or could they?

The fact of the matter is, I've never really appreciated the moniker as it has been used with Bill Clinton, I am painfully aware that Hillary Clinton is *not* her husband, and we are not living in the same times that we were when President Clinton was christened with that title.

I mean it - even now, I'm still really not comfortable with hearing Bill Clinton referred to as the FBP. Please don't start lobbing grenades, Clinton-lovers. Yes - I *am* aware of the extra lengths to which the Clinton Administration went to be inclusive to blacks, and yes, I *know* that he grew up in the Deep South and played with black children, and yes, I can remember watching in amazement with the rest of the nation as he played the jazz saxophone like an old Kansas City great on Arsenio Hall's late-night talk show. But still, there is something about referring to him as the FBP that just doesn't sit well with me. When I really stop to think about it, I think it's maybe that the idea of seeing Bill Clinton called the FBP back then, felt a little too much like we were admitting that he was as close as we'd ever get to one; as if hoping for an *actual* black president was just plain... out of the question.

For sure, in a nation where there have only been a handful of black presidential candidates (and up until now, not a single one who could have ever been considered truly viable), it's easy for many Americans to

116

believe that a President of any race other than the white race is somewhat of an impossibility. But there's a reason for that, and I'm certain it will be as hard for many to hear as it is for me to type. The reason we've never been close to running that *truly* feasible black candidate is because we've never had one who was interested in governing the *entire* nation, and not just championing the cause of blacks, and all of our socio-economic challenges. Until now. Let that sink in for a moment, and then read on.

I can remember as a younger woman, often asking myself *why* people like Shirley Chisholm, Carol Moseley-Braun and Al Sharpton insisted on wasting tax-payers' dollars and their precious time by running a presidential race that they knew they had absolutely no chance of winning. It would take years for me to understand that any delusions they may have actually had of winning notwithstanding, each of them also had as their goal, getting issues important to the black community into the national spotlight. That was it, pure and simple, especially in the case of Reverend Al Sharpton. Once I came to that realization, I understood the importance of what those candidates tried to do, and that right or wrong, effective or ineffective, it was an important continuation of the movement for equality for blacks in this country.

The need to use a run for the White House as a political stage for affecting change for the black community has come with a price, however. Now, as a result of us never having a black candidate for President who understands the plight of black communities in the context of the complex political realities of our nation, we are in danger of missing out on a man who could truly *be* the First Black President, and potentially one of the most unifying and effective presidents our nation has seen in a long time.

We as blacks have been sadly conditioned by the pseudo-campaigns of the black men and women who have made brave runs before, to believe that in order for us to throw our support behind any black candidate, he *must* be primarily a defender of the black community. I say sadly, because the harsh reality is that for us to do so is to relegate ourselves to a future with no chance of a black President, and that really is sad. As deep and enduring as many of our social problems are, electing a woman because of her marriage to a man who has nothing more than a superficial kinship with our community is a mistake. The problem with all this blind faith in Hillary is that it's really just a longing for the good 'ole days of Bill playing the saxophone for us again. But Bill is not running for President.

Please don't get me wrong. I admire Hillary Clinton, I really do - what's not to admire? She's been grooming herself for the presidency practically from the day she was born, and she's brilliant. Love her or hate her, you can't deny that, so as a woman who is constantly striving to break the glass ceiling in corporate America, I can't

118

help but admire her. But want her to run our country? Uh, not so much.

See, for me, it's all about timing. It's about what kind of leader we need now, for where we are as a nation right now. Here we are mired in a bloody, senseless war that we never should have waged in the first place, our reputation around the world has tanked, our most pressing domestic problems still plague us (healthcare, education, the AIDS crisis), and from a global perspective, we're economically at risk because of soaring trade deficits, our dependence on foreign oil, and the eminent shift of global economic might to Asia.

Billary had their opportunity to bring about change, during a time when we were far less distracted by global issues. I recall that Bill Clinton put some very cool initiatives in place while in office, stuff like the "Community Technology Centers" which were part of the effort by his administration to bridge the digital divide, but Hillary's flip flopping, her "now I support it, now I don't" dance around her position on the war in Iraq just does not instill a lot of confidence in me.

There's much more, of course - Hillary's failed attempt at reforming healthcare is legendary, and can be attributed to the Clintons' inability to build consensus across party lines. They made many mistakes in attempting to pass real reforms, like trying to tie the bill to a budget reconciliation plan, and refusing to compromise when moderate legislators suggested they should do so. A proven inability to see both sides of a debate and make tough decisions for the greater good of the nation is key in leading us out of our most serious problems. I believe Senator Obama has proven that he can and will lead justly, negotiate fairly, and perform effectively as President of the United States.

I sense that there is a distinct hesitation among some to broach this subject with Black America, but the power of "The Bill Factor" cannot be overlooked. It's going to take everything we can muster to cut through the longing and the sense of nostalgia many feel for Bill Clinton. We can do it, but only if we're not afraid to confront those who argue passionately that what we need is another chance with Bill in order to make things right. We can do it if we can stand firm and point out the obvious differences in Senator Obama and Hillary Clinton, the least of which is the fact that she's simply too polarizing a figure to be an effective leader. The absence of political baggage, the wisdom, the integrity, and the vision to unite the nation all make Senator Obama the clear choice. And that would be true even if Bill Clinton *were* running.

Fired Up, Ready to Go!

Any other year, this would be about the time that I would start popping the popcorn. Yep. This is about the time during any election season when the gloves come off, and the candidates start to duke it out "Thrilla in Manilla" style. It's always very entertaining, and most other years, I would have sat on the sidelines and chuckled a lot. Not this year of course.

Still, the fun is just beginning. Just this week, it was reported that the Clinton camp was busy manipulating questions at a "town hall" meeting, complete with hand-selecting questioners, while today, CNN is reporting that a blatant e-mail attack against Senator Obama that accuses him of being less than patriotic has put him on the defensive. You gotta love politics.

At times like these, the political wrangling seems less like a battle for the hearts and minds of the American voter, and more like a game of "who's got the best Jedi mind trick". Right about now, I'm thinking the Clinton's have the sacred Star Wars mind control method down to a science. Let's examine the evidence:

As you may recall, after a debate several weeks ago, Senator Clinton could be overheard soliciting Senator Edwards' support in finding a way to shut the other "less important" candidates out of future debates. Hill forgot to do a mike check first. The whole world heard her plotting, and suggesting that she and Senator Edwards should "talk". It reminded me of an episode of the Sopranos - I'm not sure why. Despite a temper tantrum from Dennis Kucin...Kusen - that little dude that saw the UFO - this little display of 'two-faced-edness' faded into the political ether, swept under the rug by a collective Jedi mind-meld from the Billary camp, never to be heard about again. Amazing.

Then of course this week, former President Bill Clinton could be heard pronouncing to anyone who would listen that the problems his lovely wife encountered with Healthcare reform during his administration were "all his fault". He claims that their attempt at reform failed because there wasn't enough money to fund it back then, and that this time (of course), money will flow like honey to pay for Senator Clinton's healthcare reform, because *this* time, Congress won't be out to get *him.*

Yeah right. A great, big, fat, part of my resistance to yet another Clinton candidacy is the fact that I truly believe that just as it was during her husband's administration, the guys on the other side of the aisle in Congress will be chomping at the bit to see Hillary fail, laying waste to any new attempt at medical coverage for all Americans. Let's face it - the experience that she so gleefully points out at every turn includes years of doing battle with many of the same men and women who are currently in the Congress, battles through which she and Bill barely made it through alive. I don't want the country put through another eight years of scandals and back-biting with the Clintons, and I believe their political history, the good and the bad, is best left in the past. It's time for a new day, and new leadership. I've said it before and I'll say it again, Senator Obama's ability to bridge divides to get things done makes him the clear choice for me.

My favorite Clintonian-Jedi-Mind-Trick this week though is the "he-didn't-have-his-hand-over-his-heart-during-the-singing-of-the-national-anthem-so-clearly-he-hates-America" email. It never ceases to amaze me how people underestimate the intellect of the American voter with crap like this. Are we *really* supposed to believe that with all that this man has done as a public servant, all he's done to get within striking distance of the Presidency, he would throw it all away by thumbing his nose at the nation's theme song? Even typing it feels ludicrous, and yet in an attempt to make the Senator look bad, people are spreading the email like it's got a topless picture of Brittney Spears in it. Or J-Lo. Or somebody. If my friends within the Clinton campaign would ask a poor college student to lie about the source of a question at what's supposed to be a forum for open dialog, is it really a stretch to think someone in that camp wouldn't hit 'send' on a few strategically addressed emails to get the Obama-smear-train going? Hmmmm?

And what about the scripted town hall meeting? Pretty risky gamble on the part of the Clintonistas, and unfortunately, this time they rolled snake eyes. The young girl who reported the unwanted solicitation from the Clinton campaign team to ask a question on global warming looked like she wanted to take a shower as she recounted how the campaign operative poo-poo'd the question she *wanted* to ask in favor of one from his list - one that was labeled "from young college student". Too funny!

Something tells me Ms. Front Runner is feeling the heat, and is trying to cool down the kitchen. What it also means is that it's time for us Obama supporters to throw hot grease on her kitchen floor and toss a match on it. Though at times it's easy to grow weary and want to just stop - stop canvassing, stop talking about it, stop thinking about it - now is not the time. Right now, it's time to dig way deep down within and find our second wind. And let me tell you, it will be just as hard for me to do so as it will be for anyone, because I'm plum tuckered out, but I *will* do it, because it is just too important.

The silly political tricks and parlor games that the Clinton campaign is playing only further solidifies my belief that *we must have change.* I don't want to be governed by someone that has to take money from big business, because they might not hesitate later to put the needs of their big-biz friends before the nation's. And I don't *want* to be governed by someone who can talk about their failures as if they were non-existent, because it may make it too easy for them to fail later, during a time when failure is not an option. And I don't *want* to be governed by someone, anyone, who didn't have the wisdom to know that the War in Iraq was a horrible, horrible mistake, because it makes it much too hard to trust any decision they make in the future. And that's real talk.

I want to be governed by someone with principles, who understands that he/she must lead this *entire* nation, and not just the part he agrees with. And I want to be governed by someone who has been in the trenches in the poorest neighborhoods in this nation, but who has the ability to understand from a global perspective why the United States is where it finds itself - ridiculed and looked-down upon by many of our past allies - and what we must do to repair our reputation around the world.

So no popcorn for ME this time around, no sir, this time I take action. For every goofy trick the Senator's opponents play, we should become even more "fired up, and ready to go". I know I am - are you?

Been There, Done That

Never truer words have been spoken. And yet, they were uttered tonight by one Ann Coulter, right-winged author, conservative talk show maven, spewer of untruths, and hater of the progressive movement and everything that Democrats stand for. She used the phrase "been there, done that" to describe how we Democrats are beginning to feel about another Clinton Presidency.

Amazingly, while filling in for Bill O'Reilly on tonight's "Factor" on Fox News Channel, Ann Coulter used that phrase while asking a question that so completely encompassed my feelings about Senator Obama's appeal, and Hillary Clinton's *lack* of appeal, that it what as if she'd been reading my blog. Hmmm.....

Ms. Coulter and many others in America are reeling over the news that Senator Obama has pulled ahead of Hillary Clinton in Iowa in what is a sure sign of gained ground on the part of the Obama candidacy, even though the poll numbers point to a statistical dead heat. The

November 14 - 18 poll of likely Democratic voters in Iowa showed that 30% now support Senator Obama, while 26% support Clinton. John Edwards pulls up the three-man race rear with 22%.

None of *us* at BWFO are surprised of course - there are people like us all over this nation, of all races, ages and socio-economic backgrounds spreading the word about the man who will be our next president, tirelessly canvassing, meeting in homes, and openly discussing why we need Senator Obama to get the fresh start that this nation is so in need of. No we're not surprised, but it was a hoot hearing Ann Coulter rant about it.

So what did Ms. Coulter say, you ask? Well, in seeking to understand the turn in poll numbers in favor of our favorite Senator, she asked one of her panelists (Lanny Davis, a Hillary supporter) whether or not Democrats:

- Feel like they've "been there, done that" with the Clintons
- Want nothing more to do with the scandals and back-biting of the past that we've experienced during the Clinton Administration
- Are done with not *only* the Clintons, but also the Bushes and want a fresh face
- Just plain trust Senator Obama more (which polls all over the nation seem to indicate)

...and so on, and so on, to which I of course blurted out a resounding "YES!" at my television (clear throat).

127

I think that my perspective is less than unique; I truly believe that Hillary Clinton could be a decent President, if it weren't for all the political baggage she would bring to office. Amazingly, she and the Clinton-machine have been able to spin all of she and Bill's political baggage into perceived "experience" and "effectiveness" in her role as First Lady, and that's all hunky-dory, but for me - it is about so much more than just, does she *know* how to lead. It's about would she make the *best* leader.

And of course, I feel the answer to that question is no. Actually, HELL to-the no. I was of this opinion even before I witnessed several of her debate performances, but now - I'm even surer of it. Her super-rehearsed, sometimes snide, sometimes vague responses to debate questions make her look calculating and sneaky, and *that* my friends, is what the American people are beginning to see. Through debate performance after debate performance, she has become more and more cynical, preachy, and arrogant, and all that equals mistrust to people like me, and the rest of America's voters.

The people who support Senator Obama on the other hand, I like to believe, have taken the time to get to know the man, and believe in his vision. I know I did and do, which is why I've become so deeply involved in his campaign. I knew beyond a shadow of a doubt once I got to know the man behind the candidacy, that he was exactly what America needs.

Feel me - Bill Clinton was what we needed in 1992. Barack Obama is what we need in 2008.

Some among Senator Obama's supporters say that they'd like to see an Obama-Clinton ticket. They believe that Hillary Clinton has earned the right to be a Vice President at least, and that if she can prove herself as a resourceful leader, capable of taking direction from a man of vision, and able to put behind her the scandals and missteps of the past, that she probably even deserves a crack at the Presidency one day. My stance on this is well documented, but what I will say is that no matter what she might deserve some day, *this* is not *that* day! Right now, the country needs a new leader who can bring a fresh perspective to the issues that are plaguing us, and who will be respected and admired as he works to repair our reputation around the world.

So yes, Ms. Coulter, for once you got it right. Been there, done that, gave away the t-shirt on the Clintons. And yes, this is a pivotal day for Obama supporters, a day worthy of celebration, but also a day during which we should remind ourselves that poll numbers mean nothing when we're *down* in the race, and they mean about the same when we're up. There is much more work to do, and six weeks left during which fortunes could change if we let our collective guard down, and so rather than see today's events as a sign that we can slow our political roll, we must keep working to build on the momentum and keep doing the work that got Senator Obama where he is today in this election.

For Black Women for Obama, that means a special focus over the next several weeks on South Carolina. As Tori Scarborough, the South Carolina coordinator for "Women for Obama" shared with me just this week - we *must* do well in the early states, of which (of course) South Carolina is one. Our fight in Georgia is coming, but right now we're needed in the S.C., so that's where we'll be.

So cool to be part of a winning team.

It's Time for the Fun Part?

Considering what the Clintons had to endure during the eight years that Bill Clinton was in office, you would think that they would find political attack-dogging anything but "fun", but that's how Hillary Clinton described her reportedly stepped-up efforts to shine a negative light on Senator Obama.

If like me, you believed all along that Hillary's status as the presumptive nominee was destined to pale, you know that the kind of crap that we'll soon hear coming from her campaign was inevitable. My favorite zinger-fallen-flat so far *has* to be the, "see - he's ALWAYS wanted to be President, uh, uh, look at page 269, paragraph 7 of his book! He said it when he was a KINDERGARTNER! See! Senator Obama was trained to be a cunning political strategist before he barely even knew his alphabets!"

Ludicrous. What does it serve the American people to know that Senator Obama once aspired to the Presidency practically as a toddler? Hell, I've already announced to the world that my 10-year old, one David Isaiah Smith, will be the fourth Black President of the United States someday, but only God, the creator and finisher of his destiny knows for sure what he will become. The bottom line is, Senator Obama was called to lead, because of a passion for service, his intellect and knowledge of our government and it's laws, and because it *is his destiny*. Pure and simple.

Now, of course, the campaign is attacking his pro-choice stance. In the passage that follows, which was sent out today by Becky Carroll (the National Director of Women For Obama), it's plain to see that some of the very people who have now united to try and tarnish the Senator's record were the same ones who once stood with him, and even celebrated his allegiance to the Pro-Choice movement:

Dear Friends:

The campaign is heating up, and Hillary Clinton is resorting to old-school political attacks in a last-ditch effort to slow Barack Obama's growing momentum.

With new polls in Iowa showing Senator Obama moving into the lead -- and ahead with women voters by 5 points – Senator Clinton and her campaign are shamelessly attacking Barack's record and his character.

Just weeks after Senator Clinton promised not to attack her Democratic opponents, yesterday she announced that she would enter a new period of daily attacks on Barack, going so far as to say this is "the fun part" of campaigning for the presidency.

The problem with Hillary's attacks is that they're filled with false charges and desperate rhetoric. First, she falsely claims that Barack Obama doesn't support universal health care, even though he has a detailed plan that would provide affordable health insurance for every single American and do more to cut the cost of health care than any other plan in this race.

Then her campaign attacked our youth empowerment efforts and tried to intimidate Iowa college students who plan to participate in the caucus. They even published an article on their website attacking Barack for telling his kindergarten teacher he wanted to be president when he grew up.

Now they're trying to attack Barack Obama's 100% pro-choice record.

Today's attack was delivered by Ellen Malcolm, President of EMILY's List – which has endorsed Senator Clinton and is spending millions on an Independent Expenditure campaign to try to get her elected. Malcolm called into question Barack's commitment to protect women's rights by pointing to old votes on a few politically motivated bills in the Illinois Senate. What

Malcolm failed to point out was that Barack cast these votes as part of a strategy employed by pro-choice leaders in Illinois. That's why so many top pro-choice leaders were outraged by the attack and immediately defended Barack's record of leadership on this important issue.

Not only is Senator Clinton's claim another baseless, desperate attempt on her campaign's part to distort Barack's record, but this tactic does nothing more than divide the pro-choice community at a time when we need to work together to elect a pro-choice candidate for president.

But don't take our word for it. Read what leaders in the pro-choice community – who have worked side by side with Senator Obama – had to say about the latest Clinton attacks:

"I am a supporter of Hillary Clinton and an EMILY's List donor, but this line of attack is unacceptable. While I was the president of Chicago National Organization for Women, Senator Obama worked closely with us, could not have been more supportive of a woman's right to choose, and there was no bigger champion in Illinois on our issues. What's important is that the candidates do not cannibalize each other on issues we all agree about because we need to win in November." Lorna Brett, former president of Chicago NOW

"During his years in the state legislature, Barack Obama was a strong and consistent supporter of women's reproductive rights. He worked hand-in-hand with Planned Parenthood in developing and executing strategies to make sure that women had access to reproductive health care. I also want to thank him for standing up with us in the effort to open the Aurora clinic and for his introduction of legislation guaranteeing access to low-cost birth control. Planned Parenthood/Chicago Area has proudly endorsed Barack throughout his entire political career." Steve Trombley, CEO & President, Planned Parenthood/Chicago Action

"The present votes Obama took at that time, along with many other pro-choice legislators, were 'no' votes to bad bills being used for political gain. We asked Senator Obama and other strong supporters of choice to vote present to encourage Senators facing tough re-elections to make the right choice by voting present, instead of caving to political pressure and voting for these bad bills. In the Illinois State Senate, Obama showed leadership, compassion and a true commitment to reproductive health care. The Republican Senate President at the time constantly used anti-abortion bills to pigeon-hole Democrats so that he could target them with misleading mailers during campaign season. It was a tactic that was about politics, not policy - and Obama didn't let them get away with it." Pam Sutherland, President & CEO of Illinois Planned Parenthood Council

"Senator Obama is one of America's strongest and most loyal defenders of women's rights on issues of reproductive health care. I've contributed to EMILY's List in the past but I never will again, because I'm so disappointed in their decision to launch these unfair, false attacks on behalf of Senator Clinton's campaign."
Libby Slappey, a former 13-year board member of Planned Parenthood of East Central Iowa.

Even Ellen Malcolm has praised Barack as recently as last year, after Barack gave the keynote speech at the annual Emily's List Luncheon. In a letter to Barack, Malcolm writes:

Senator Obama,

Thank you so much for helping to make the 2006 EMILY's List Majority Council Conference such a great success. Our Majority Council members told me again and again how energized they were to hear directly from you and how much they appreciated your spending time with us.

You truly inspired our members and reminded them why they support our work to elect dynamic pro-choice Democratic women especially after hearing you speak about how you're fighting to make change happen.

I appreciate your commitment to EMILY's List. Here's to victory in November!

Warmest regards, Ellen R. Malcolm, President

Handwritten: "You were terrific and really lit a fire with our members!

Thanks so much!!"

These attacks are not going away any time soon. Let's be sure to remind ourselves and our friends about what a fighter Senator Obama has been for the pro-choice community.

· Barack has a 100% pro-choice vote rating with Planned Parenthood and NARAL Pro-Choice America.

· He was the ONLY U.S. Senator who helped raise funds in 2006 to successfully repeal a South Dakota law that banned abortions. Senator Clinton refused to help in the effort. In fact, even EMILY'S List refused to help repeal the ban in South Dakota.

· Senator Obama is the only candidate for President who rose in support of Illinois Planned Parenthood when their new Aurora clinic faced a threatened shut-down.

· When Congress failed to pass a law to require insurance plans to cover FDA-approved contraceptives, Obama supported a successful law to provide that requirement in Illinois.

· He recently co-sponsored a bill with Senator Claire McCaskill (D-MO) to make birth control more affordable for low-income and college age women after changes in federal law led to a skyrocketing new costs.

Please share this information with your friends and colleagues. Let's make sure that these kinds of divisive, baseless attacks don't go unanswered.

Becky Carroll

More politics as usual. I understand, as I'm sure every American does, that heated political discourse is a necessary discomfort in the electoral process, but when it borders on the ridiculous, like this whole kindergarten thing, it makes us all just feel, well, less than intellectual. As a matter of fact, the more I read some of this stuff I think, the dumber I get.

Luckily, Senator Obama's campaign has all of this covered, so the rest of us are free to do what is needed most - contribute our time and efforts towards getting out the vote, and spreading the word about the need for change in this country. So let's push past the ridiculousness of the recent campaign rhetoric and speed the Senator from Illinois along to victory in '08. The work is ours to do, and it will only be done if we do it.

Fired up and ready to go?

One Historic Day in South Carolina

It was a beautiful, sunny Sunday afternoon. The sky was brilliant blue, and the only way you knew it was December that day was because, well, you just knew.

I waited around for my assignment outside of Columbia's Williams-Brice Stadium along with the rest of the volunteers from Atlanta that had rode on the van I had commandeered on behalf of the campaign. The truth of the matter was it didn't matter to us *what* we did to help; we were there to be part of history.

The campaign had been forced to move the event that some were calling "The Big O" from its original location to the huge college football stadium after tickets for the original venue were scarfed up after only three days. It was clear to most that South Carolina planned to come out in huge numbers to see a famous talk show host named 'O', but that they would also be there to find out more about Senator Barack Obama and what he's all about.

And that was amazing enough, you see - if
you know like me and a lot of other volunteers in South
Carolina know, you know that not so long ago, not very
many ordinary people in The Great State even knew who
Senator Obama was, let alone that he was running for
President. It would take campaign offices and
personnel, stationed strategically all around the state,
working side by side with volunteers from neighboring
states, all tirelessly stumping to get the word out about
the Senator to make the difference. And on that
exhilarating day, on the 9th of December, all the work of
those faithful foot soldiers had paid off.

There were thousands upon thousands of people, lined
up around the block long before doors were due to
open, there to witness what would turn out to be an
historic event - the day that Oprah Winfrey, a cultural
icon who until then had *never* formally endorsed a
political candidate, had come to speak to South
Carolinians about why she had chosen to break her self-
imposed political silence for Barack Obama, and no
one else.

Amazingly, since Oprah has been out on the road with
Obama, some of her 'devoted' fans have taken to
castigating her on her website. She's suddenly being
accused of 'playing where she doesn't belong', and
'forcing her political will down the throats of her fans'.
Those who make these baseless accusations do so mainly
because they have somehow come to believe that the

only reason Oprah has chosen to back Barack Obama is because he's black. Incredible.

Only those who refuse to see the deeper meaning in an Obama presidency would cheapen what Oprah did that day in Columbia and before in Iowa by saying that she's only endorsing Senator Obama because he's black; Not only does such an inference cheapen the importance of that day, but it also belittles the work that Senator Obama has done, the man that he is, and the President that he is destined to become. It also says some pretty unfair things about Oprah Winfrey herself.

The most prevailing quandary created by the Obama candidacy is the dichotomy it exposes regarding race relations in America. I've said many times in this forum that as a black woman, I have repeatedly been accused of supporting the Senator because he's black; I've heard other blacks criticized for *not* supporting the Senator *even though he's black.* It's positively mind boggling - at the same time, Senator Obama has been called 'not black enough' to win the support of African Americans, and 'not electable' in the eyes of mainstream America. His bi-racial heritage has been criticized as proof that he could not possibly understand the African American condition, and held up as proof that he alone is uniquely qualified to understand the changing face of America and our place in the world.

Even our black leaders dare to rob him of his 'blackness' in favor of a man who is not black, was not the 'First

Black President', could never *be* black, and who only
garners the ridiculous comparisons to black
Americans because he's been so vilified by what most
consider his unacceptable behavior in the White House.
No need to say his name.

And so a man like Senator Obama who has by his ability
to unify across racial and political lines in his campaign,
already proven that we have made truly historic gains in
race relations in this country, has also by doing so, shone
a bright and blinding light on how far we have yet to go.

So what then, of the over 30,000 mostly African
Americans, who stood patiently in lines that snaked
around the stadium to see the most famous black woman
in history, talk about the only African American in
history who has a real shot at becoming the leader of the
free world?

I thought of them all as I stood a few feet from the stage
and surveyed the assembled crowd; they sat mesmerized
as first Michelle Obama, then Oprah Winfrey, and then
Senator Obama himself offered words of hope for the
nation and the outcome of the election. I smiled at the
sea of faces, as Senator Obama painted a vivid picture of
what the future could hold for our country, if we dared to
believe. And before long, I began to realize that because
of Senator Obama's strength, because of him and
Michelle's ability to push past the naysayers, the race-
baiters, and the discouragers, what I was witnessing was
a true and earnest turning point for South Carolina

and for America. I was witnessing the dawn of a new era of politics that if allowed to take root, would once again respect and uphold the idea of government for the people and by the people, and that if allowed to flourish would uplift and include instead of tear down and exclude.

Just like everyone else in the stadium that day, I was there to hear the man whom I believe is truly the only one who has the vision, the strength of character, and the sound judgment to be the next President of the United States. But I also noted with pride that in some way, I had played a small part in helping to get those people to that place, with my phone calls, my endless blogging, and my crowd control skills :). I had been part of an amazing team that day that through our collective belief in the audacity of hope had helped to make that day possible.

So as I stood mere inches from Senator Obama and Oprah Winfrey as they enthusiastically shook the hands of those in the crowd, all I could think was, "How cool is this?" And "God Bless America".

An Awesome Responsibility

This is Iowa-Caucus Day, and I can't help but reflect as I bop around the site what an awesome responsibility it is to play a part in this nation's political system.

And the caucus system makes it even more daunting. For those of you who may not know, the Iowa caucus has been the first major electoral event of the nominating process for President of the United States since 1972. It has served as an early indication of which candidates for President might win the nomination of their political party at that party's national convention.

This year, of course, is particularly exciting and historic, as it seems almost certain that either the first black man or the first woman will be nominated as the Democratic Party's choice to run for President. It is a very cool time to be alive, in so many ways!

For starters, there is no doubt that we are experiencing a political renaissance in this country; most people, out of necessity, have begun to actively participate in the process, either by paying much closer attention to the issues, or by getting up and out and doing the work for the candidate of their choice. For me, that choice is of course Barack Obama; for you, it may be someone else, but all indications are that more people than ever before in history are taking an active part in the political process, and that is historic in and of itself!

As a nation, we have so much at stake - a war that should never have been waged, children being lost forever in the education system, Americans without adequate healthcare, our nation losing the technology race, and an ever worsening reputation around the globe - the man or woman who becomes the next leader of the free world will inherit an office and a set of problems unlike any other before him, and so we need a leader who has all that it takes to bring the country through it.

What issues are important to you? Have you already made a decision about whom you'll support? If you (like many Democrats) are locked in a vacuum of indecision over Obama and Clinton, what hesitations do you have about both? Have you done YOUR due diligence to make sure you know all you need to know to make an informed decision?

There may never be as historic and important an election as the one of 2008. The future of our nation, our very ability to remain the super power we have been for so long is at stake. It is so easy for us to lead our comfortable lives, cozy in the fake knowledge that things will just 'work out', and believing that someone else will make the moves to ensure that. But ask yourself this - can you imagine being one of the people who did NOT get out and vote in 2004, when it was critical that we get Bush out of office? Can you imagine what it must feel like now to know that if you'd just gotten out and voted and encouraged others to do so that you may have actually *saved the lives of some of America's servicemen and women?*

That's real talk. So this election year, make sure to let your voice be heard. Go to the polls during your primary or caucus, and before the vote, get involved in getting out the vote in your community! Start with your home, then move to your church, your job, and then out into your neighborhoods, but do everything you can to ensure that the voiceless are represented, and that the voiced open their mouths and collectively pull the virtual lever on the ballot box. Only then can we rest assured that we've done all we can to make this nation a better place in which to live.

And wouldn't that be worth it?

The Meaning of Change

Anyone willing to bet what next year's 'word of the year' will be?

I'm guessing it'll be 'change'. Since Senator Obama's decisive win in the Iowa caucuses this week, I don't think I've ever heard a word uttered so much by so many. The cable news pundits, the candidates themselves, the focus group members, my family members, strangers on the street - all talking about 'change' as if it were some sort of new age cure for everything that ails us.

What strikes me as most interesting though, is that the other candidates in the Democratic field, namely Senators Clinton and Edwards, hardly knew how to spell the word before January 3rd, and yet suddenly, they're both proclaiming themselves as professional change agents, and the only ones who could possibly bring about the transformation that Iowans proved the nation so desperately wants.

There's only one problem - neither of them seems to understand what real change *means* to all of us, and unfortunately for them, the concept can only really be defined by the ones for whom change is most important - the American people.

Hillary Clinton in particular has begun to screech about affecting change in a shrill and insistent way that makes her sound like a spoiled teenager trying to convince her parents that she's ready to date. On several occasions since the Iowa Caucuses, her main battle cry has been "it takes experience to bring about change", and that she effectively has been 'making' change (as if there's some magic recipe book for it) for the last 35 years. And that's where she has gone sorely wrong. Or at least where she's pretended to.

During the ABC News/Facebook debates tonight in New Hampshire, Hillary could be heard at one point impatiently exclaiming (and I'm paraphrasing), "if balancing the budget and improving the economy is not making change, then we all must have some kind of amnesia!" I cringed for her - I literally wanted to hop a plane to Manchester, grab a cab and dash over to St. Anselm College, fight my way past the Secret Service, dive for the stage, drag myself to where she was sitting and give her a hug. It was at that moment in the debate that I realized that when it comes to the subject of change, Senator Clinton is clueless, an unwitting victim of her own denial, backed into a corner with no way out

- and what's worse - she doesn't even know how she got there.

It's as if she doesn't see what's 100% obvious to everyone else. By handing Senator Obama the decisive victory that they did, Iowans made it patently clear that they wanted to be the ones to usher in a new political reality, one free of the baby-boomer, Vietnam and Watergate era politics that created the divisions that exist between the citizens of this nation today. One that is inclusive of the everyday American, and promises an earnest attempt at unification for the greater good of the people of this nation, rather than more of the same partisan sniping and bad judgment that has left our global reputation in shambles, our military weakened and fighting wars for no reason, and our collective political spirits broken. A new political age that only Senator Barack Obama has been able to convince us is possible, and that only Senator Obama has helped us dare to dream of.

The kind of change Senator Obama can bring about has little to do with pure policy, though heaven knows that for the last eight years we have been saddled with a myriad of policies by the Bush Administration that have been disastrous on every imaginable level. Further, the kind of change Senator Obama can bring to office represents so much more than anything getting in a time machine and heading back to the nineties, or trying to enact the same old failed Clinton initiatives can bring. Senator Clinton rants about the changes she can make because of her perceived breadth of experience, because she doesn't understand that the change that we long for, the change that Iowans clearly showed they want to see has to do with not *what* we do as a nation, but *how* we do it. It runs deeper than either she or Senator Edwards (or even Bill Clinton for that matter), is capable of understanding, as proven by her knee-jerk reaction to her 3rd place showing in Iowa.

The numbers bear it all out - Senator Clinton may have won the majority of votes from older Americans, but in practically every other category that mattered - women, younger voters, independents - she was left in the dust by Senator Obama, sputtering, and wondering what the hell had happened. Fortunately for me, as a loyal Obama supporter from way back, I can tell Ms. Clinton *exactly* what happened. Senator Obama has somehow single-handedly managed to challenge a new generation of thinkers to imagine what kind of nation we could be if we would be brave enough to shake off the shackles of the past, and abandon the notion that we *can't* communicate with enemy nations, or talk to our neighbors who are not of our same political affiliation about the problems that plague us. We've all been conditioned to *not talk to one another, ever.* We've been conditioned to believe that real, meaningful discourse is not possible across political aisles, and that no leader could possibly work with members of the opposing party to do what needs to be done to fix our nation's ills. We've been conditioned to view our nation through a murky, dirty glass, which Senator Obama has shown us can be

150

cleaned, and polished, and made bright again, so that we can all collectively begin to see a brighter future for this country. He's challenged us to imagine *real change*. And Lady Hillary just doesn't get it.

It's probably not her fault. Senator Clinton can only see what she's been doing for all those 35 years she brags so much about. All she can see is the political maneuvering, and the polls that direct her actions - like the ones that told her that she *must* talk about change now. It would be nice if someone in her camp could get her to slow down long enough to explain to her what change really means to the brave citizens of Iowa and to the nation. I'm not going to hold my breath though.

It's best if those of us who get it just remain steadfast, and undaunted by the Clinton's attempts to yet again scramble for a bandwagon in order to align themselves politically with what the polls say they should. They've not fooled anyone so far, certainly not Iowans, and I'm betting that New Hampshire will see right through them as well.

It makes me wanna sing hallelujah - it's a new day! Hillary and Bill Clinton's day is over, and our future looks brighter than it has in a very long time. It's too bad that we'll have to endure more dry debates, primaries, and stump speeches before we get to that glorious end, but the bottom line is that we've come too far to turn back now, and it will be SO worth it. Thank you Iowa, for creating a defining moment in my life, one that I will tell my grandchildren about one day, one that I can proudly say I was a small part of. And thank you for showing that America is still the greatest nation in the world, capable of reinventing itself even during the most difficult of times. Aren't we lucky to have the architect of that reinvention right here, right now, ready to one day lead us all, black, white, young, old, Democrat, and Republican, by standing on the world stage and proudly proclaiming to all who will listen that "America's back"?

It Takes a President

Faithful readers - by now I'm almost bored with pointing out when Hillary Clinton steps in her own poop, but I have to weigh in on this one. It's too important.

Unless you live under a really big rock that doesn't have cable, you know that this week during an impromptu Fox News interview, Hillary told a reporter that:

"Dr. King's dream began to be realized when President Lyndon Johnson passed the Civil Rights Act of 1964. It took a president to get it done."

Now, this morning CNN is reporting that Hillary and Bill are in full damage control mode, doing the news show rounds, and accusing the Obama campaign of "distorting" her words regarding Dr. King. As if we've all been inflicted with some sort of collective brain disorder that renders us incapable of hearing and comprehending on our own. Sheesh.

I hate to be the one to break it to Hillary, but there is no going back on this one, and African Americans around this country are correct to be incensed. What she said was not taken out of context, it was not misinterpreted, and none of us have heard incorrectly. Hillary Clinton thinks that Martin Luther King Jr.'s efforts during the Civil Rights movement were just "a dream", and that it took Lyndon B. Johnson, a politician, to swoop in and make his and the dreams of millions of socially, financially and physically abused Black Americans a reality. Wow.

What a terrible misstep. Even I, someone who is no fan of Hillary Clinton, and who really just wants the Clintons to fade into history, don't really believe that *she* really believes that Martin Luther King Jr. had no substantive part in the Civil Rights Movement. Only an idiot would believe that, and Hillary's no idiot. But are we distorting her words? Heck no. She said what she said when she said it, and now she must be made to pay the political piper. Hillary Clinton has proven yet AGAIN, that in the heat of the moment, when her back is against the wall, she'll say and do *anything* to try to portray herself in the proper light. So in trying once again to do so, whether she meant to or not, she dismissed the historical importance of the man who without argument *was* the catalyst, visionary, and leader of the Civil Rights Movement in this country.

It's mind-boggling. What Hillary said to that reporter makes her seem like someone who just doesn't understand the power of a *movement*. That's the real problem. At a minimum, in stating that Lyndon Johnson was really behind the change that occurred during those perilous years, she once again has shown that she just doesn't understand what any of us means when we talk about *real change*. And at worse, if she really DOES believe what she said that day, then she really is the soulless being people portray her as, and so entrenched in the Washington political machine, that unlike another famous 'matrix', the biggest red pill in the world won't snap her back to reality.

If Rosa Parks had never stayed seated on that bus that day, if Reverend King had never inspired the masses to protest the injustices of that time, if Malcolm X had never stood up to say that we will achieve our freedom in this nation "by any means necessary", if all the other fighters, the ordinary people of that time had not organized, marched, chanted, listened, rallied, and worked tirelessly to change hearts and minds - President Johnson would never have been moved to act. Period. Get it now, Hillary? Lyndon Johnson may have put his blessing on the law with the stroke of a pen that finally legally validated what so many people fought and died for (including of course Dr. King), but it was the architect of that movement, and the many everyday citizens who would not take no for an answer that made it happen.

Now - enough of Billary. I want you to dare to dream with me for a moment. Imagine if you will that the architect of the *new* dream of a truly United States actually *was* the President. Imagine what it would be like if the man who was challenging the nation to think of what we could one day be, unified, together, working to tackle our nation's problems as a collective rather than as a group of labels actually occupied the Oval Office. Imagine if he had not only *taught* us that the dream is possible, but was actually in a position to make that dream a reality.

In Senator Barack Obama, we're going to have *both* an inspirational leader and a courageous chief executive, and *that* my friends is what this nation both wants and needs. We want to be inspired; we want a moral leader, someone who can step up on the world stage with courage, free of scandal, political baggage, and the shackles of a history of self-aggrandizement, ready to say what needs to be said, and do what needs to be done to solve the nation's and the world's problems.

So let Hillary and Bill waste their time with their endless political rants. We know that we have so much more to look forward to in Senator Obama. Unlike the Clintons, Senator Obama is not the least bit interested in twisting or distorting anything in the hopes of getting the desired reaction for the moment. And that's why he *will* be the Democratic nominee, and the next President of the United States.

One more thing - any African American that votes for Hillary Clinton after this doesn't deserve to benefit from all that Dr. King and our forefathers fought so hard to give us. Pass this one along.

An Open Letter to America

Dear America,

We are in a pivotal and historic place. Over the last several years, we have become a nation that is openly chided by those who used to be our allies, for our lack of restraint, and over-zealousness when it comes to using our political might.

We have turned our backs on our children. The high school drop-out rate in some areas of our country is as high as 52%, and 15-year olds from Poland, Luxembourg, Finland and the Czech Republic all have higher rates of math literacy than ours do. China now leads the world in the number of university graduates, and we don't have enough highly skilled workers to fill the jobs and provide the innovation that will ensure our place as the technological leader we have always been into the future.

We have lost the ability to build and maintain strong families. We have no moral grounding. Our leaders have by their example sent a message to the nation that it's okay to do anything you want as long as you don't get caught. Hypocrisy is the norm and no longer the exception and our leaders by their behavior have kept us mired in scandal and have been an embarrassment to us before the rest of the world.

We have lost control of our borders. Our lust for cheap labor has resulted in a torrent of immigrants who, though hard-working, have taxed our resources, degraded the quality of education our teachers are able to provide our children, and made the process of legal immigration seem no longer necessary.

We are saddled with a healthcare system that continuously fails us; we leave innocent children to die at the whim of big healthcare conglomerates, and our elderly have to choose between medication and food. Even those who provide most of our jobs in this country, small businesses, are having a harder and harder time affording coverage for their workers.

Worst of all, we have seen our political process descend into chaos, rendered immobile by a level of partisanship and polarization unlike any we've ever known. And so the problems that plague us, the social and economic puzzles we desperately need to solve continue to confound us, because we *cannot seem to unify to find solutions*. Our politicians seem to care more about holding on to power than what's best for our country; they lend their attentions to the highest bidder, and leave the American people to fend for themselves, unsure of how to change things, but certain that our Government is not working and can't help us.

America - it doesn't have to be like this. We *can* work together to solve our most pressing problems, we *can* be the leader in educating our children again, we *can* rebuild our families, strengthen our borders, and fix our failing healthcare system, but not if we continue to try to do things the way we've done them in the past. Doing things the way we've done them in the past will only ensure that we will *not* have the brighter future that we long for.

America - it is so much easier to fight than it is to love; It is so much easier to doubt, than it is to find the courage to change; and it is so much easier to cling to the past than it is to have faith in the future, but as a nation, we have NEVER done what was easy. We have never let people who only have their best interests at heart try to dictate ours, whether they be from other nations, or from within. As a nation, we have always found our greatest strength when we've banded together, each and every one of us to rise to a higher purpose. Well that time is now, America. It is time for us to find the bravery to shake the shackles of the past; respectfully acknowledging that our past leaders have been what we've needed *in the past* but that it is now time to begin to build our shining *future*.

160

What that means to you America, is quite frankly up to you. For me, it means having the courage to elect a leader who can step into office on day one, unfettered by the ghosts, scandals and baggage of his political past. A leader who has demonstrated by his example a fervent desire to give the government back to the people, and who has no sense that the nation is obligated to elect him to office for no other reason than he (or she) says it should be so.

For me, it means having the courage, and the wisdom, to elect a man who has himself exhibited profound courage and wisdom in the face of attacks from the most skilled and organized political machine this country has ever known. Because I love this country, and everyone who lives in it; because I *know* that we are meant to turn towards a brighter future, and not stay mired in the past; because there is no other way to repair the damage that has been done by the familial dynasties that have had a strong hold on our political system for almost thirty years, I will do all I can to ensure that Senator Barack Obama becomes the next President of the United States. I'll do it for you, I'll do it for myself, but most of all, I'll do it for my eleven-year old son. It's just too important.

It is our job to leave our children with a better nation, a stronger one than we found, America. The kind of nation that only a new perspective, fresh ideas, and honest to goodness unity can bring about. I am not afraid to let go of the past, America, and you can't be either.

Love,

Patricia Wilson-Smith

The Crisis in Kenya

Imagine it - you're a three-year old. You're awaken in the middle of the night by the sound of men wielding machetes, and all you hear as you cower next to your bed in terror are the screams of your family, as the violent strangers kill them one by one. You survive only because you go undetected. You've survived - but now you're all alone.

You narrowly escape the fire that the strangers set - you stumble out of your home, onto the street, half-dressed, nearly blinded by your tears and the heat of the fire, and you watch as your home, and everyone and everything you hold dear in it, is ravaged by the flames.

Imagine then that this scene is repeated day after day after day for weeks - and that it seems to go on without end. This story and others like it are being repeated in Kenya today, even as we all sleep soundly in our nice comfortable beds, and worry about how we're going to pay our Dillard's bill this month.

On December 27th, an historic Presidential election was held in Kenya, one in which the Luo had hoped to see one of their own, Raila Odinga, elected to the highest office in Kenya for the first time.

Early polls showed that his victory over Mwai Kibaki was imminent, but greater than anticipated turnout in Kibaki strongholds, where the Kikuya live seemed to magically erase any pre-election lead for Odinga, and Kibaki was sworn in as Kenya's President. Again.

The result has been an outbreak of civil violence and unrest that had once only reared its head in the nations surrounding Kenya. At last estimation, over 350,000 men, women, and children have been driven from their homes by the violence, and machete-wielding warlords had taken the lives of over 1,000 Kenyans.

There has been no real outcry - not from around the world, not from within the United States. We watch the sparse coverage of the story on the nightly news, and click our tongues, and turn the channel to get our daily Election '08 fix, forgetting that the man who is responsible for sparking the political imaginations of so many, the man who has taught us all that as a nation, we can hope for more tolerance, more patience, and more unity, has his roots in Kenya, still has family in Kenya. We are connected to Kenya, whether we want to believe it or not.

It is so easy for us to live our daily lives, secure in the knowledge that no matter how bad our economy may get, no matter how disillusioned we become with our political system, our society will never disintegrate into chaos or anarchy, because, well, it just won't.

But today, in Kenya, hundreds of thousands of people who live in the once tranquil, tourism-rich nation are now fleeing for their lives, leaving behind decimated homes, and any sense of safety they may have known. Can we really stand idly by, knowing that so many people are dying, and living in fear, and that no one is lifting a finger to help them? Would we be more willing to help if Kenya sat atop a great oil reserve, or if they were a strategically important base of operations for the U.S. in some other way?

What if a sea of phone calls could make the difference? What if you could copy this passage, cut and paste it into an email, send it to all of your friends, and make a difference?

Well maybe you can. I urge you, all of you, to make a phone call to your local television stations, your elected officials, your friends, your families, and anyone else you can think of, and remind them that the ancestral home of the man who has proven to be our greatest hope for a unified nation is under siege and needs our help. Kenya needs our help. It is time for us to see beyond ourselves, beyond our own borders, and help where we are needed, whether we have interests there are not.

Join me in contacting someone today - anyone, and telling them about the crisis in Kenya, and asking them to make a call to their congressman or Senator, and demand that they do SOMETHING before it's too late. If you can't do it for the Obama family, then do it for the innocent Kenyan children - they have everything to lose, and nothing to gain from the violence that threatens to destroy their land.

There are a number of great organizations lending their voices to this cause. If you'd like to learn more, or to make a donation, go to http://relieforkenya.blogspot.com - it has links to a donation form, as well as posts about ongoing activities in Kenya.

Is It Time for Hillary to Step Aside?

I came across the letter recently, and I thought I'd share it.

A former Clinton supporter wrote this open letter to the Senator from New York on February 14th. It is moving, and eloquent, and dead on:

(Source: http://www.clintonsupporters4obama.com)An Open Letter to Hillary Clinton, By Erin Kotecki Vest

This is a very hard letter for me to write, so please bear with me.

I'd like to ask you, with all due respect and humility, to step down as a Democratic Candidate for President of the United States.

Please understand this is not because I believe you cannot or should not lead this nation. Please understand that I find you qualified, capable, and worthy. Please

167

also understand I want nothing more than to see a female as the leader of the free world. I would be pleased and honored if you were that female.

However I am finding, right or wrong, many citizens of this country seem to react to you on an emotional level. Emotional, not practical. They can't seem to see your record. They can't seem to see your policy. They just hear or read "Hillary" and venom or praise spews.

I thought that with your candidacy, would come reason. I thought that you would be able to get a fair shake by main stream media, by voters, by sexists, and by soccer moms. I thought over time people would begin to see that you really are an effective politician.

I was wrong.

Tonight, I'm typing as I watch you speak in El Paso, Texas. I'm sad. There really is no other way to put it-I'm sad.

I truly believed you would be the best person for the job, and I had this nagging thought in the back of my mind that is now at the forefront. The thought that drove me on Super Tuesday to Vote for Senator Obama and the thought that is the driving force as I write tonight: Senator Hillary Clinton divides this country.

It's not fair. It's not right. And under just about ANY other circumstance I would go to the mat for you.

168

However we are a wounded and deeply divided nation. We are a nation at war. We are a nation at odds with each-other. It's ugly. I thought you could get people past it. I really did.

When I told myself it was gender that got people going, I refrained from asking and wanting you to step aside. Simply on principle, I wanted to see you run and win because they said it couldn't be done. Because it was my belief, this was all about being a girl.

It's not, and I was wrong.

I firmly believe while the gender issue has given you a handicap I hope we all one day overcome, it is NOT the reason people have a gut reaction to you or your campaign or your legacy.

Enter the Senator from Illinois, and what I think could be your true legacy. If you were to step aside now, shockingly early and shockingly un-Hillary-like, you could galvanize an entire nation behind your party. If you were to throw your weight, and your tremendous political clout behind Senator Obama you could still change the world and make your mark in a way no one would expect and everyone would admire.

I don't want to see you throw in the towel because the fight is too hard or the mountain too tall. I am asking you to throw it in because history is on the line. It is not the history either of us expected, however it is an equally important, momentous, earthshaking change in this country we sorely need.

Do something no one would ever expect. Do something extraordinary. Do something that changes politics as usual and changes history.

I could have never predicted having to choose between what my husband called "the lesser of two goods, not the lesser of two evils" when it came time to cast my vote.

It was agonizing.

But in the end, with no major policy difference and valid reasons on BOTH sides, I had to go with the candidate who I thought could best bring our nation back together. Who could cross party lines and gender lines and racial lines.

I wanted it to be you, but it's not. For some reason you still get people very riled up, and not in the good way.

There is no way around it-it sucks. But after 7 years of nothing but fighting and head shaking and feeling like we're living in two Americas, I can't do it again. Not even if my team is in office.

I really hate asking you to do this, but I want you to please step down and let this nation heal.

We've been too angry for too long and your history and your name brings a suitcase of anger to the White House front door.

With the full weight of the Clinton name, behind the scenes, your true legacy could be written. With the full weight of the Clinton know-how you could help orchestrate the next chapter in American history where an African-American leads our nation.

It is this time in history your nation needs you.

As nation's go, ours has never been one to do things the way we predict. Who could have seen when we finally get our first, legitimate, female front runner we'd see our first, legitimate front runner of color?

Our nation and its people need you to do what is best for this country. We need you to be true to what you say on the stump and bring us back together.

If you firmly believe that there is still time for you to change the hearts and minds of those rude and stubborn Americans who are voting with their gut when they see "Hillary" on the ballot-then please, prove me wrong. I'll be at the Democratic National Convention come August and I'll hold up my Hillary sign loud and proud and fall in line.

But I think you've tried. You tried with everything you had to overcome that Clinton-emotional reaction. Here

171

*we are, moving into Texas and Ohio and Pennsylvania-
and it's not you winning over hearts and minds, it's the
Senator from Illinois.*

*Let's end the division in this country now. Right now.
Let's start with the Democratic Party early and provide
a united front against the GOP months ahead of
schedule.*

*Let's take back this country for the people, with you
playing a much different role than you envisioned.*

Make history. Make us one. Step down now.

Sincerely,

Erin Kotecki Vest

Is Hillary likely to read this letter, break into tears
(again) and order her top campaign aid to immediately
draft her concession speech? Not likely. But the writer
frames the argument for why she should do so, so well
that you can't help but wish that somehow this letter
could be hand-delivered to the lady herself.

Those who seek to minimize what's happening in this
country say that we Obama supporters are 'voting with
our emotions' and that we support Obama because 'he
makes us feel good'. What ELSE are we supposed to
vote with when we've been mired in a pointless war for
years, when our economy is teetering on collapse, people

172

are losing their homes, teenagers are dying at the whim of huge medical conglomerates, and the likely nominee of the Republican Party wants us to stay in Iraq for 100 years?

What these people don't get, these pundits who think they can psycho-analyze the American people, is that Senator Obama has moved us to action, and not just tears, and that can NEVER be underrated. There is a fever growing throughout this country, even Hillary supporters feel it, as evidenced by the growing number of defections from her camp. We want to be part of history - but not just the history that will come from electing our first African American president. I for one want to be part of this time in history that years and years from now will be described as the time when men and women of all ages, races, religious persuasions, and yes, even political affiliations truly and for the first time became the United States of America.

Super-delegates: Who the F%$*k Knew!

Okay. I consider myself an intelligent woman, and I am nothing, if I am not forthcoming. So I'm going to admit it to everyone. Right here, right now, on BlackWomenforObama.org. I had NO IDEA that Super-delegates existed before, oh, say a month ago. Got that off my chest. Whew! I feel a lot better!

What I want to know is, am I all alone? This election season has been historic in that it has drawn more people into the political process, and not just in a passive way, but in a way that has gotten people like me truly engaged, and getting engaged means becoming aware of some inconvenient truths. If you're like me, you know that the REALLY scary part is, the more we learn about our electoral system, the more broken it seems. And that's not good.

In a nation that prides itself on barn-storming communist or socialist or dictatorial nation states and cramming democracy down their throats, I'm a little baffled over how the Democratic and Republican parties could have thought that the super-delegate system was a good idea or even remotely in line with what our fore fathers had in mind when they gave every man the right to vote (unless you were black - that's another subject entirely). I mean, seriously - do YOU think the signers of the Declaration of Independence really meant for us to vote, march, rally, demonstrate, make our will known, all so that 800 seemingly randomly chosen people could pat us all on our collective heads and do whatever the hell they want? I don't!

And yes - I'm using expletives liberally today. It is no friggin' wonder that the political establishment is scared to death of Senator Obama - he's dragged most of us kicking and screaming into the Matrix! He gave us all pleasant-tasting blue pills to suck down, and we thought we wanted them, and now we find out that the Matrix is running our political lives, and that we have much less control over who we elect as leader of the free world than we thought! Amazing!!!!

Think of it - what will we look like to the rest of the free world, let alone evil dictatorships, third-world countries and the like if we elect Senator Barack Obama as the Democratic nominee by popular vote, and 800 of the 'chosen ones' in this country end up going, "Nah, we don't think so. He's a hope-monger. Hillary - do your thing". I submit that our status as the freest nation in the world will be called into question, and our credibility will be shot. Again.

So what can we do about it? At this point, just pray. Pray that Hillary Clinton will want to avoid an ugly showdown at the convention. Pray that someone wins by a large enough margin that no showdown is necessary. Pray that Howard Dean can pull a rabbit out of his hat if things start to go awry. Pray, pray, pray.

As someone who is newly addicted to all things political, I have to say that though I'm disillusioned, there is an upside. Now I want to know what ELSE I've been bamboozled, run amuck, and led astray about. I mean, what's next? A hidden tax? Independence Day is really December 25th and Christmas is really July 4th?!?! I mean, sheesh, is anything what it seems?

Only time will tell. Thanks to Senator Obama in large part, the eyes of millions of Americans have been opened to the possibilities of what one person on a mission can do, when they band together with the like-minded. My hope is that the leaders of the Democratic Party and the candidates themselves will endeavor to do the right thing when the time comes. But if they don't? There's always revolution. And yes, it will be televised. Take THAT Fox News!

Barack Hussein Obama: A Name You Can Trust

Who wouldn't want to give their child two names that have such beautiful meaning: Barack means "blessed" and Hussein means "good; small handsome one"?

John Campanelli, DailyKos.com

This week's flap over the use of Senator Barack Hussein Obama's middle name in the media is the subject of this week's rant.

Earlier this week, a conservative talk show host (whose name I refuse to use here) kicked up a lot of dust by yelling Senator Obama's full birth name over and over again during a tirade disguised as an introduction of Senator John McCain at a rally. This guy swaggered back and forth in front of the cameras like a man grateful for his fifteen minutes, showboating in front of an audience of about 7 people, and spewing some of the most racist crap I've ever heard on the national airwaves.

His goal was to remind the American people that we are in danger of electing a man to our highest office that shares a name in common with a dead dictator. He also took it upon himself to spout the normal right-wing platitudes about how the Senator would handle the economy as President, and how un-safe the nation would be.

This would have all been pretty laughable if the news media hadn't become so transfixed on this moron for days afterward. They loved it - they ate it up! This freak of nature was featured on every national news program there is for almost a week, and each time he took a new opportunity to display his hatefulness and blatant bigotry.

The irony is, I think his lunatic ramblings did serve a purpose. It both exposed the still deeply engrained racism that still exists with many in this country, and forced us all to deal with an issue that would have eventually reared its ugly head anyway - whether or not to use Senator Barack Obama's full given name when referring to him, as we have done in the case of every other President in our nation's history.

It took me only three seconds to figure this one out. After watching this race-baiter in action, I quickly realized that we should not only use his full name, we should all counter this idiot by collectively shouting it from the rooftops!

Barack Hussein Obama! Barack Hussein Obama! Barack Hussein Obama! I want it plastered on all of his campaign signs, and I want every political pundit at CNN, and every lusty news wench at Fox News to let it fall from their lips whenever they refer to him. Why? It's simple - because we cannot as an electorate say that we support Senator Obama as the Democratic nominee for President unless we are willing to support him in his totality, and that includes his name.

If you think about it, this is an amazing opportunity - this is, in essence, America's big final test. So many of our fellow citizens have been able to see past the efforts of those who would have stopped Senator Obama's candidacy in its tracks because of his name AND his race. They've been able to see through the veiled efforts to paint him as 'the black candidate', and as an inexperienced demagogue. Surely we can also live with the fact that there is more than a real likelihood that our next President coincidentally shares a name with a man who by all accounts was a murderous monster!

It's time to face facts. Senator Obama is, as of this writing, on the brink of staging the greatest political upset in modern history, and all we have to do America is pass this one final test - all we have to do, is learn to love and respect the name, like we love and respect the man. I know I can do it, and I also know why.

My 11-year old son, David, is named after his father, David, who walked out on me when I was four months pregnant *on our wedding anniversary* and never looked back. At the time, I named my son David because I sincerely believed that one day I'd find a way to put my family back together. When I realized there was no hope, I begin to rue the day I'd decided to name my gorgeous, beautiful son after his father. Those early days were truly miserable.

But guess what happened? Can you guess? That's right! My love for my son soon faded any memory of the pain his father caused me, and eventually his father became someone who just happened to be named after my son, rather than the evil owner of the name I once prayed I could forget.

Saddaam Hussein was an evil, murderous tyrant. Jeffrey Dahmer ate people, but I don't go running in the other direction when I meet someone named Jeffrey, no more than I hide my wallet and the weapons in the house if someone named George happens to stop by. It's time to face it - there is a very real possibility that Senator Barack Hussein Obama will be the next President of the United States, and when that happens, those who are uncomfortable with his ancestry won't be able to avoid his middle name any more than they can avoid his black skin. Those of us who have until now turned a blind eye to the uncomfortable realities of his birth name won't be able to avoid it either, so it's time to face it head on, and take it for what it is - God's way of showing us that there can be beauty and honor even in the things that remind us so much of what's wrong in the world, like my son's father's name once did. It's an opportunity for us to tell ourselves as proud Americans, and to tell the world that we really are the fair and just nation that we so deeply want to be, capable even of lifting to the highest heights a man with arguably one of the most infamous middle names ever.

Yes - this is our final test America. We have shown that we can all push past our prejudices to embrace the hope of a different America - our prejudices about the ability of a black man to win the White House, our prejudices about whether or not a country with such a racially peppered history could accept him as a candidate at all, and yes, our fears and biases over his rich ancestry that is so different than ours, and that is so evident by his name. A complete and total acceptance of Barack Hussein Obama is the only way we can truly embrace the change that his presidency will bring to our country, and the only way we can begin to shake the racist shackles of our nation's troubled past.

The Definition of Representin'

I wrote a book a couple of years ago called "Duped By Love", and in that book, I had a great time making fun of how the media here in the A.T.L. loves to walk the streets of the worst neighborhoods, looking for stuff to report on, and trying to find the least articulate person on the planet to interview about whatever newsworthy thing has taken place.

Don't act like you don't know what I mean.

A young black man is a witness to a drive by shooting, and describes what he saw with a heavy dirty South accent. A middle-aged black woman witnesses a domestic disturbance, and through barely decipherable English, recounts the tale to the reporter and camera man who have her framed against a background of urban desolation, eager to exploit her for the amusement of their audience. I HATE that crap.

There is no denying it - in cities and states around the country, the news media make it a point to seek out those that they feel will portray the black man, woman, and sometimes even the black voter in the worst light possible. Enter Derrick Ashong and a CNN reporter known only as "Mike".

On January 31st, Derrick Ashong, a 32-year old musician found himself pulled into the fray of the Democratic debate being held at the Kodak Theatre. He was talked into standing outside the event and holding an Obama sign by a good friend. Now, it must be noted, that to look at Mr. Ashong is to see nothing particularly special. Outwardly, he looks like any other street kid, and if we were to be 100% honest with ourselves, he has the exact look of someone that some people might cross the street rather than confront face to face for fear of being robbed or worse. Yes - outwardly, Derrick Ashong could be the poster child for the image of young black men that the media has taught the viewing public to fear.

So I'm fairly certain it was with this (and ratings) in mind that a CNN cameraman/reporter walked up to Derrick Ashong and asked him pointedly, and rather rudely *why* he supports Senator Obama. I'm ashamed to admit, that when I was first told to watch the video, and the first few seconds rolled across the screen, I felt a certain discomfort over what was coming.

You see, in an age where people often amuse themselves by recording each other's most idiotic moments and publishing them to YouTube for the entire world to see, I was certain that what I was about to be treated to was more of the same. I can distinctly recall that I felt that pang of dread that I often feel when viewing some new example of blatant black stereotyping by the media. I felt it, yes I did. But I sat there and made myself watch, and I continued to listen - and what I saw and heard brought pure joy to my heart.

Mike the CNN reporter hammered Mr. Ashong with probing question after probing question about why he was standing outside the Kodak Theatre that day in support of Senator Obama. At first, Derrick gave a few canned answers that sounded suspiciously like something you might pick up from Obama paraphernalia. And so Mike probed more deeply. He asked Derrick about the candidates' health care plans, how they would be funded, he asked him about socialized medicine, and the likely economic impact of an Obama healthcare plan - and as the questions grew more complex, Derrick Ashong proceeded to school both Mike the CNN reporter *and* me on the superior aspects of the Obama plan, and why it makes the most sense for the nation.

And it's not just that he beat back an obvious attempt to make an Obama Supporter look substance-less - he did it with so much finesse, authority and in such a knowledgeable way, that the reporter had no choice but to allow himself to be drawn into an engaging conversation with a young man who was obviously his

184

intellectual equal, and abandon what I am convinced was meant to be an opportunity to show the world that young black men, and the youth of this country in general are rallying behind Senator Obama like the unwitting victims of some pied piper, or like groupies to a rock star. Wow.

Derrick Ashong single-handedly destroyed about half-a-dozen stereo types in the space of 6 minutes during that interview. He proved, first, that young black men do much more than sit around smoking weed all day waiting for opportunities to rob and loot, as is so often portrayed in the media. Secondly, he showed that even the very young can be extremely well-versed in the issues of the day, and knowledgeable of the candidates they support. Thirdly - in casually announcing that his father was a pediatrician, he showed the reporter that young black men can be the product of good homes, headed up by educated professionals, and that not all black men standing around on a street corner come from broken homes.

Fourth - he shattered the myth that the typical Obama supporter is just somehow 'in-love' with the Senator, or only on the campaign's bandwagon because Senator Obama makes good speeches. Fifth - he proved that even someone who has made a conscious decision to be a musician can still be politically engaging, and an intellectual. Sixth, he dispelled the myth that young voters don't understand what's at stake in this election - I could go on and on and on.

The bottom line is, it seems like lately, every day in every way, we are beginning to get the proof that our nation is turning a corner. We are beginning to really get a flavor for the power our diversity gives us as a country. You see, Derrick Ashong is an immigrant from Ghana, educated here in the states. He is young and passionate, but old enough to recall that there was a time when he lived in a land where he did not have the right to vote. His command of the issues was amazing, his enthusiasm for Senator Obama clear. The reporter repeatedly (at first) chided him about providing 'technical' answers, and not just 'emotion' to support his positions. So in the face of what most would consider to be grilling on the part of the CNN reporter, he kept a cool head, and stuck to the facts.

The video of his interview that day has been played on YouTube by hundreds of thousands of people, and has become so popular that he's been accused of being an Obama plant, which is ridiculous when you think about it. But to answer the naysayers, he produced a follow-up that he calls 'The Emotional Response', and if the first video impresses the heck out of you, this one will move you beyond belief.

In it, he discusses his love for this country, his unique ethnic background, and his appreciation of our democracy. He talks about why it is so important that we figure out a way to get past our differences, and come together for the good of our country. Sound familiar?

The beauty and the power of what occurred outside the Kodak Theater that day cannot be overstated. Out there that day, two men, one white and one black, bridged both an age and racial chasm, to find common agreement on an important political issue. What happened out there that day? Without trying to, one young man showed America the face of yet *another* black man who cares more about the collective well-being of our country than he does about any singular racial or socio-economic group. What happened was that Derrick Ashong validated what Senator Obama has often said in his writings and in his speeches. "I know they're out there", he says in the *Audacity of Hope*. "Those people who are tired of politics as usual, and want a different kind of politics". He showed America that not only are they out there, but they might show up in the most surprising ways, wrapped in the most unlikely packages.

Thank you Derrick, for being the very definition of 'representin'.

History: A More Perfect Union

Wow. The blogosphere is ablaze. Everyone is giving
their two cents on what I'm convinced will go down in
history as the "I Have A Dream" speech of our
generation.

Unless your television or computer was carried off by a
twister (Atlanta caught it in the neck from a record
number of tornados last week), you know that today,
Senator Obama delivered an historic speech on race
relations in this country, and the controversy that made
the speech necessary - the remarks made by his former
pastor, Reverend Jeremiah Wright.

I am utterly amazed at how eloquent some have been in
their analysis of Senator Obama and the historic speech
he made today in Philadelphia, and yet how utterly
wrong at the same time. The thing that stands out
the most to me is the many bloggers and their assertions
that Senator Obama was somehow deeply conflicted or
panicked as he delivered his speech today. I find that

odd, because I didn't see conflict or panic in him at all. I saw resolution, and a bravery that is seldom seen in modern politics. Those who are busy accusing Senator Obama of tap-dancing to get out of a sticky situation missed the point of his speech entirely.

America - listen to me. The easy, political thing for Senator Obama to have done would have been to stand up, and bang the podium, and say that he forever disowns, denounces, rejects, and otherwise dismisses his relationship with Rev. Wright. That would have been the easy AND politically expedient thing to do, and I'm not sure many people would have blamed him for it. But instead, what he did was deliver a message to the American people that was long overdue, for black and white Americans alike - the message that the things that have divided us for so long will never go away unless we find the courage to confront them.

And in confronting this issue with his Pastor, he showed us by example that confronting the issue of race relations in this country can and should be done, whatever the consequences.

Check it - I am the quintessential Obama Supporter, and yet I must confess that had I been one of his advisors, I may have been tempted to ask him to take a different road than the one he took today. There had to be a burning debate amongst his strategy team, if not inside the man himself - *was it more important for Senator Obama to say what was politically acceptable, say*

whatever would get him back in the good graces of the
majority of Americans, or was it more important for him
to show himself to be the truthful, profound leader that
he has portrayed himself to be all along, by telling the
American people the truth, even in the face of such an
ugly controversy?

This question is not as easily answerable as you might
think. Certainly, there are those who desperately want to
see Senator Obama as the next President of the United
States who might be tempted to say that he should have
said whatever would make this thing go away the fastest.
These are the people who believe that the political end
justifies the political means, even if the means forces
someone of honor to do the dishonorable.

And they are wrong. Dead wrong.

What Senator Obama had the courage to stand up and
say today, well, right now we're all just marinating in it.
The pundits are batting it around, the hard-core Clinton
supporters are ringing the death knoll on Senator
Obama's continued chances, and the Republicans are just
sitting back giggling at the spectacle. But I would
contend that what we as a country do today in response
to Senator Obama's message hardly even matters,
because so historic was his speech, so important was the
message, so sweeping in its delivery of the facts of the
state of race relations in this country were his ideas, that
it was actually worth running the risk that it could throw
us all off kilter for a bit at best, and seriously jeopardize

his candidacy, at worst for the American people to hear it. Sorry for the run-on sentence.

See, the people who really love this country and want it to turn a corner, are willing to sacrifice even our selfish wishes for our country's future in the name of truth. And what Senator Obama said today was the truth, whether we wanted to hear it, whether we liked it or not. And the most amazing thing is that there was enough truth in his remarks to go around to everyone, blacks and whites. I felt a distinct sting when he began to talk about how blacks play the victim over racism in this country at times, because he was right. And I felt a definite discomfort at his assertions that some whites don't seem to understand that the residual effects of slavery are still being felt by blacks in this country today, because I know he's right about that too, but I also know that so many people are just not ready to hear it.

Some have suggested that he didn't want to deal with the pastor's comments until he had to. To that I say, "Duh!" The people who believe that are absolutely right - of course he didn't deal with it until he had to, and the reason is that he knew that it would be something just like this that would force him to have the discussion with the American people about the state of race relations in this country. And he knew that the message he would have to deliver would be hard to say and hard to hear. But I applaud him, a million times I applaud him, because what he said today was the bravest thing that any politician in recent memory has had to stand up before this nation and say, and it was probably also one of the hardest oratories a politician has ever had to deliver.

It saddens me that as a nation of intellectuals there is so much we can't seem to agree on, whether we're black or white. Today, I saw a man put everything on the line to tell the truth as he sees it. I saw the Senator stand up for a man who he loves - though he doesn't agree with his more controversial remarks AT ALL - and respects for those qualities that have served he and his family well over the years. And I saw a man that in a million years would never wish this country harm. In that there is no question.

But sadly, other people like the maniacal bloggers who are ripping him to shreds even as I type saw what they wanted to see - a racist, or liar, or whatever other names they've chosen to call Senator Obama since he left the podium this morning.

But ask yourself this - who is it who throughout this campaign has consistently thrown mud, and distorted the truth, and used surrogates and her ex-pres husband to say or do whatever it took to cast doubt on her opponent? Who is it that has done everything possible to stoke the flames of racism in this country, just to gain political advantage? And who has consistently gone on record as not wanting to engage in gutter politics, not even to revive his candidacy or ensure victory for himself? And yes - who is it that stood up today in front of the

American people and spoke from his heart about his deepest fears for our country? Who reminded us of what should have been patently obvious to anyone who has picked up an American history book - that slavery was a blot on our nation's history that left a terrible, enduring stain? And who was it that did it possibly at his own political peril?

You know the name. Say it with me. O-B-A-M-A. This country needs the leadership and honesty that Senator Obama showed today, nothing else will do if we're to ever leave the generations of racial division, hatred, and confusion behind. I for one long for the day when asking questions about someone's racial motives is as passé as asking about their shoe size. I have faith that that day will come, and that when it does, Senator Obama will have lead us there.

Hope Changes Everything

Hope really does change everything, doesn't it?

If you're like me, you remember the early days of the Obama campaign, when hope was all we had. We were Obama supporters before being Obama supporters was cool, back when it was one thing to *know* that we saw in him a quality that was unmistakably presidential -and quite another thing to think that one day he would be on the brink of actually becoming the Democratic Party's nominee.

But we had hope. Hope that the nation would one day see what we saw; hope that neither his race, nor his age, or any other superficial deterrent would get in the way of the Senator's rise. Hope that the greatest political machine in our nation's history could somehow be neutralized in order to fulfill our dream of an Obama presidency. Hope.

But the hope went far, far beyond just the Senator's electability. As we, the soldiers of the early days made our way from house to house in the hot South Carolina sun, or stood in line waiting to see Senator Obama speak long before stadiums were necessary to contain the crowds, we also hoped for a new unity, one born of the need to move our nation in a different direction; away from failed Bush policies for sure, but also, away from a divisiveness that our partisan politics and class-warfare had only made far worse.

And so we met up with other Obama soldiers, and we planned, and we worked. Black women stood shoulder-to-shoulder with young white men and painted signs; elderly black men rode vans with Asian college students, and traded stories, sang songs. And slowly but surely, we realized (as Senator Obama put it), that we were in fact not nearly as divided as our politics would suggest.

It's been an amazing ride, and it's not over yet. Black Women for Obama has made a small mark on the political landscape, by proclaiming early and often that there was no moratorium on our vote, and that we believed even before the rock-star receptions on college campuses that Barack Obama was and is destined to become the next President of the United States. Not because he is a rock star, but because he's rocked our collective political worlds, by teaching us how to look to the future as a truly united nation, and how to begin the work of leaving the past that still haunts us where it belongs - as a reminder of where we've been, but no deterrent to what we can become.

I have fallen madly in love with Senator Obama - sorry Michelle, it had to be said. He has renewed my faith in politicians, men, basketball players, and religion. He has reminded me that it was in the black church that those who came before me found the strength to fight for the liberties I now enjoy, and made me realize that it's okay to "do me", and not cling to the crutch of past racial injustices as I make my way in the world. But most importantly, he has taught me that I actually do have a voice that can grow as loud as I dare dream for it to. He has deepened my appreciation for democracy, and reaffirmed my belief in what's possible in this nation that I love so much. He deserves my undying love for that reason alone.

And so, let's face it - this journey nears its end, and through the light at the end of the tunnel, I can see a huge, red, white, and blue sign that reads, "Barack Hussein Obama, the 44th President of these United States". And each day that the Senator's opponent fudges the truth, fakes the numbers, and continues to play transparent political games, my view of that sign grows a little clearer. And so hope, in practice with works and faith, becomes a vehicle for change, real honest to goodness change. And all I can ask myself as I sit here happily typing away is, "When the inauguration is over, and it's time to get down to brass tacks, what will this nation dare to hope for next?"

Weighing In On Reverend Wright

For those of you who may have wondered why I've been largely silent on the Rev. Wright issue, here's the truth - the whole thing has been way too disheartening for me to deal with head on. Until now.

Because now I feel I have to. Any of us who has a voice, even a small one, who does not loudly weigh in on this debacle will be as culpable as the media and the Clintons in Senator Obama's defeat, if such an unlikely thing were to occur.

I am an educated black woman, who was raised in the black church. I have black family members and friends who have strongly held views on everything from slavery to whether or not as consumers we can truly influence the price of gasoline. And as I have walked the streets in support of Senator Obama, I have heard from more than my share of blacks their frustration and disgust over what they perceive as an endless history of injustices brought down on the heads of people of color by this country. Some I have spoken to have achieved some semblance of the American Dream; some still struggle to gain ground on even a meager existence in this country. They're Americans - they pay taxes, and they work hard, but they're fed up, and sometimes just as controversially vocal about it as Reverend Wright has been.

Some that I've spoken to along the way have said from the very beginning that "America is not ready to elect a black man President". I can remember hearing those words, and thinking that those people were so short-sighted. Especially in the glow of the Senator's huge win in Iowa; I vehemently defended this country and the people in it, saying that Americans were changing, and that Senator Obama was the kind of man who could bridge divides that had long existed, that he was uniquely qualified to do so. And let's face it, he has done that - and if all things had been equal, I believe Senator Obama would already be the nominee. But instead, me and people like me are left scratching our heads, wondering how it is that at this late date in the primary season, when Senator Obama has won more pledged delegates, more of the popular vote, and more states, we could possibly be pondering the possibility of a Clinton upset, all because of a preacher who not unlike thousands of preachers around the country both black and white, takes political and social license with his sermons on Sunday.

It's appalling. Despite my desire to believe differently, I can no longer deny that in giving this story life, and continuing to breathe life into it on a daily basis, the media has put Senator Obama in a position to have to defend the one thing that he cannot and should not have to - his blackness. All because of the irrational fears that some have that he might hold some deep-seated resentment for this country that might someday pepper his policies should he become President.

Now, I'm afraid that any black man who dares run for high public office will always be vetted on a much deeper level; that the fear-mongers will always contend that SURELY an educated, politically successful black man must harbor some festering anger that will somehow show itself eventually! Never mind that our current President dumped us head-long into a war that there is no clear way out of (a war that Senator Obama was wise and sound of judgment enough to oppose from the start by the way)! Never mind that the Republican candidate has a temper that he doesn't even try to hide, and that Billary have proven themselves to be congenital liars and political opportunists so selfish that they don't care if they destroy the Democratic party to win the nomination - Senator Obama is black.

Senator Clinton has definitely done her part to keep the Rev. Wright story alive, but at this point, I have to place the blame for all this firmly where it belongs - on the media. I think what gets me most about all of the non-stop media coverage of Rev. Wright is how show after show after show keeps asking the same questions about which sermons Senator Obama heard and didn't hear. How they keep playing the same clips of Reverend Wright over and over again, giving a ridiculous amount of attention to the perspective of one man (who by the way is not running for office), without lifting a finger to get to the real heart of the matter. The fact is, the media has done more to perpetuate the unfounded fears Americans have about Senator Obama than anyone else, and that includes the Clintons. And in doing so, they have put our dirty racial laundry out in the open for the entire world to see. Left unchecked, the media will be guilty of robbing this nation of the opportunity to re-invent itself in the eyes of the rest of the world; it will cause events that will disillusion the millions of young voters who have been awakened, and who now recognize that their future depends on our ability to break the political log-jam we've been in for decades. If we don't do something soon, the media will rob us of our first chance in a long time to have a truly great leader.

It is clear by now that it is easier for the media, and others in this country to believe that Senator Obama, a man who has proven himself time again to be a unifier, is somehow really some angry black man, bent on making the nation pay for its crimes against humanity. Rather than see the Harvard-educated family man, legislator, and community organizer, they would rather use those with whom he's associated to diminish him into some caricature of a man that is white America's greatest fear. To believe the truth, to believe that we are actually witnessing the candidacy of a man who has what it takes to transform the way we think about ourselves as a nation, and who has the courage to force us to look at ourselves in an honest, truthful way is just too much for some. And so now, I'm thinking that those early naysayers might have been more right than I wanted to believe, and that makes me so sad.

It boggles the mind - are we really supposed to believe that all the work that Senator Obama has done over the years, working in poor neighborhoods, when he could have gone straight to any high-dollar law firm in the country, toiling in the Illinois State Senate, working tirelessly to bridge divides between the left and the right when he could have just as easily become a partisan yes-man - was all so that he could eventually become President of the United States of America and foist his deeply hidden divisive and racist political views on the country?!? Is THAT what we're all supposed to believe?

It's amazing that it's come to this, especially at the hands of the Clintons, because when it comes to character, Hillary Clinton is the polar opposite of Senator Obama. During the ABC debate in Pennsylvania hosted by George Stephanopoulos and Charlie Gibson (and I use the term "debate" loosely here), we learned once and for all what kind of man Senator Barack Obama is. The two moderators, armed with a myriad of pointless questions to be directed at Senator Obama regarding controversies long dispelled, lobbed only one tiny stink bomb at Senator Clinton regarding here blatant Bosnia-sniper-fire lie, then gave Senator Obama an opportunity to slam her for it. And he could have. Some say he *should* have. But instead, he tossed their bait back into their faces, opting instead to plead for a return to a real debate about the issues. I was stunned. I was awe-struck over the magnanimousness of his response, and I was reminded anew of why he must become our next President.

But unfortunately, we continue to be so distracted by the spectacle of a Rev. Wright, and by the zigzagging polls, and the hundreds of pundits and endless cable news interviews, that we've completely lost sight of where we are as a nation and what we're trying to become. Meanwhile, people are suffering through a broken economy, a new surge in violence in Iraq has produced the bloodiest month for U.S. soldiers in almost a year, and our reputation around the world and our ability to compete continues to erode. But there's something else that hasn't changed - when asked again and again whether or not this nation is headed in the right direction, Americans have responded with a resounding "no". The problem is, due to the political skill of the Clintons, and the voracious appetite the media has for salacious stories, many Americans have been tricked into believing that it's perhaps safer to go with the lying, polarizing, do-anything-to-win-because-I-deserve-it, candidate than to have faith in the purity and hope of Senator Obama's vision. And that is just sad.

But - even though there is an unmistakably bitter, stinging tone to this piece, I still have hope. Because I know that the media, though very influential, cannot by itself turn the will of the American people. I know that the Clinton machine is running scared, having been knocked off its axis by a movement, one fueled by the longing this nation has for unity and truth in its politics, and the desire to be proud of its leader again. And I know what YOU should know - that the Republican party would rather face a dozen Hillary Clintons than one Barack Obama, inspirational leader, record-breaking fundraiser, young, brilliant, energetic political force that he is. And so to allow ourselves to let the media, the Clintons, or anyone else move us off message, or deny us what we know is best for this country, would be a much bigger travesty than anything Reverend Wright could ever serve up in his pulpit.

North Carolina, Indiana - make it right. Don't let the media tell you how to think, or how to cast your vote. It's time to end this, and it's time to end this now, for the sake of the party and of the country. Senator Barack Obama *will* be the next President of the United States, and we *will* begin to bridge the divides that have held us back as a nation for so long, but only if we are collectively brave enough to stop the madness that has engulfed us over the past several weeks. Knowing the true nature of Rev. Wright and Senator Obama's relationship will not help me reclaim the job I lost through down-sizing just days ago. And it won't help my friend, whose company closed its doors without notice last week in order to file bankruptcy. It won't help anything, or anyone - only a real leader with the bravery to tell the truth, do things differently, and stand up to the political bullies that we've been saddled with for too long can do that. And I don't have to tell you who that leader is.

See You At The Finish Line!

I have to admit - at times, I have been just about ready to shoot myself in the face over this nomination process.

I can't quite tell whether or not I've been antsy because I've never been this engaged in a nomination fight before, or if this really truly has been the world's longest primary race, or race of any kind in fact. I guess I could delve into Wikipedia to try and gain some historic perspective, but damn-it, I just don't have the energy.

I think the most amazing part of being so deeply interested in the happenings of this particular race has been watching the cataclysmic shift in the political power base, and specifically watching Billary go kicking and screaming into their joint political sunsets. I don't think anyone could have imagined a year and a half ago that we would be about to witness the bitter end of the Clinton era, and everything that entails. I don't think anyone saw it coming, especially not the Clintons themselves - the ushering in of a new day, rife with so many possibilities. I also don't think anyone could have predicted how really truly enlightening the whole thing would be - how many bright hot lights would be shone on so many things and people who I'm sure would rather have continued to dwell in the dark.

Let's see - you have the Bush Administration, just recently being 'outed' by Scott McClellan, who essentially in one fell literary swoop, validated everything that the nation has slowly on its own grown to know about Dubya's White House, and it's shady and reckless dealings. It feels to me like a pretty rare moment, when a consummate administration insider breaks under the pressure of his own conscience to cast such damaging aspersions on a sitting President - and just in time to save us from a possible third term at the hands of a man who thinks it was all okay. Whoa.

And of course you have Billary - and the take-no-prisoners, leave no truth standing approach to power grabbing that they've been accused of for so many years by the political right. I cannot tell you how many Rush Limbaugh litanies I've sat through during which he described the Clintons and their tactics in terms that at the time seemed petty, sarcastic, exaggerated, and otherwise unbelievable. As I re-play some of those snarling recitations back in my head now, I have to admit that the guy had a lot of it right. Much to the Clintons' chagrin, the power of the media, the Internet, and technological advancements in general have made it possible for each and every one of their campaign-trail transgressions to be vetted and broadcast and bandied about in near real-time for every rabid blogger and every news organization in the world to guffaw about. I mean, even with my deep disdain for Ms. "they-shot-at-me-so-I-deserve-to-be-President", I can't help but believe that she honestly just didn't realize how easy it would be for someone to produce the very footage of the Bosnian event that she tried to re-write in her many retellings of the story. A Jedi-mind trick gone awry, and all because of a tragic underestimation of the power that is access to instant information.

Then there are the lunatic ministers - Hagee on the right, Wright on the left, and so many others somewhere in between, who in doing what has in the past come so naturally (and without repercussions or consequences) have managed to create an entirely new discussion about Religion and Politics, Religion and Race, Religion and Gender (I thought Michael Pfleger's imitation of Hillary was hilarious, by the way), and Religion and well, Religion. Are we better off because we all now know what some who claim to be purveyors of the Gospel, spreaders of the good news of the deity of their choosing, etc., also may have dangerous opinions, and way too much power through which to spread them? This is a question that I think we'll all begin to ask once the dust settles, and President Obama is busy about the business of running the country; but for now, still only a question.

But finally - we have the colossal, glaring spotlight that now shines on the failings and missteps of the Democratic Party rule-makers. If we hadn't been thrown head-first into what now feels like a never-ending nominating process, would we have ever been alerted to the disastrous and possibly even unconstitutional methods by which the Democratic Party has decided to select its candidates? Most certainly not!

Yep - these have been truly illuminating times, and it's not over yet. This week will be one for the history books. This week, we resolve the issue of "hey, those votes don't count - no wait, I need them, so uh, yes they do!" This week, your favorite Senator and mine will almost assuredly be rewarded for playing by the rules, and running one of the most honorable campaigns on record when he overcomes the remaining 45 delegate deficit to secure the nomination. And this week, the nation takes a historic quantum leap towards electing a non-white-male to the presidency of the United States. I'm awe struck.

It's been tough, though. So many days and nights of political disagreements, phone calls, events, road trips, etc. Now that I'm on the other side of this thing? I feel like, hey - if as a nation we were forced to suck down a blue pill and open our eyes to the realities of our churches, our political process, and our society in general, then so be it. No matter what happens from this point forward, this race has changed the nation forever - we've seen the Matrix, and we can never go back now. The only thing left for us to do is don the cool black outfits, slick our collective hair-do's back, and begin to do the work that will turn what we realize now is a flawed reality into the one we long for. The one that Senator Obama has proven by his historic candidacy is attainable.

It has been tiring, emotionally draining, exhilarating, and yes, ever-so frustrating, but now that we're in plain sight of the finish line, I think we'd all have to agree, it's all been so worth it! Black Women for Obama loves you, America! See you at the finish line!

Fox News' Post-Racial Train Wreck

I have a stunning confession to make.

Prior to my activities as an Obama supporter and volunteer, I was a closet Fox News fan.

My affinity for Fox News began a few years back, when CNN was still a doddery, boring news channel, struggling to stem the tide of defections to the then new and exciting Fox News Network. I thought I was 'different', and 'hip' for watching the new upstart, and let's face it, Fox News did usher in the age of cool graphics, cutting edge shows, and opinion-based journalism that now reigns supreme even at CNN with the likes of Lou Dobbs (cringe) and Anderson Cooper (yummy).

Please don't get me twisted - I understood even then that their reporting was totally right-leaning, and often chuckled to myself at the notion that they were 'fair and balanced' even as I laughed at their on-air antics, but what can I say? I just really liked the on-air personalities and the fancy graphics. Pretty colors.

Also, because Sean Hannity had been a radio personality here in Atlanta, I'd followed his career all the way to Fox News. The show he did here was of course most definitely right-winged, but he at least seemed level-headed in his discussion of the issues of the day, and I saw nothing in him that seemed *unfairly* biased at all. And so, when he eventually made his way to Fox News, and well, blew up, I understood and even appreciated his success.

It all of course started to change when Fox News' coverage of Election '08 kicked in. I was amused by Hannity's "Stop Hillary Express", because it was proof positive that like the Clintons, the boys at Fox never saw Barack Obama coming. And so I was of course not surprised when as it became apparent that Barack Obama would be the Democratic nominee, Fox and Sean Hannity decided to turn both barrels on him. It was then that I began to drift over to MSNBC and CNN to check out what was happening on the political reporting front, and it became patently clear that Fox was, let's just say, a bit biased in its reporting. I went cold turkey on them then, because I wanted to hear only the positive news about my candidate for one, and also because I realized just how far the other cable news networks had come in retooling their shows, their on-air personalities, etc., to become more entertaining and informative while I had been languishing at Fox News.

What I did NOT see coming was how crazed the folks at Fox would soon become over the prospect of an Obama presidency, and the desperate, almost manic zeal with which they would soon begin attacking Senator Obama and all things African-American in order to sway the American people to their way of thinking. It would almost be funny if it weren't so....unfunny.

For me, it all boils down to Fox News holding Senator Obama to a higher, more ridiculous standard than they ever would any white candidate. From their railing on about the absence of a lapel pin of the American flag on his suit jacket (when there is scant little evidence that ANY of the other candidates ever wore one) to their insistence on repeatedly running photos of him wearing Kenyan garb and using it to question his allegiance to radical Muslims - Fox has clearly and unfairly tried to strike fear in the hearts of the American people with this kind of rhetoric. But that's only the beginning. The kind people of Fox News, and the myriad of pundits with which they associate have proven over the course of the last several months to be not only inconsistent standard bearers, but borderline racists, who are either actually panicked over the prospect of a black man becoming President, or doing a damned good job of making us all think they are.

Case in point - what the hell is a 'terrorist fist jab'? When I learned that blonde bomb shell and Fox News host E. D. Hill had uttered these ridiculous words to describe the fist-pound (as the mainstream media has NOW come to call it) that Michelle and Barack gave one another on the night that he clinched the nomination, I was mortified. I think it would have been perfectly appropriate to tease the Senator and his wife about what some might view as an unconventional salutation, but to characterize it as a 'terrorist fist jab' was just - dumb and racist. Period. And I guess I really didn't want to believe that the guys and dolls at Fox were stupid racists - I wanted to believe that they just had strongly held views about their politics. Silly me.

Then of course, we have the 'Fox & Friends' crew, lamenting for a full TWO HOURS over Barack's assertion that his grandmother was a 'typical white person' when he described how she might see people on the street that she might fear; this as news reports were breaking regarding the breach of the candidates' passport files by Justice Department employees, and right after Senator Obama's historic speech on race. It was like they hadn't heard a single word of the speech, or chose to ignore its relevance. Either way, so blatant was their coverage that day that even Chris Wallace - himself a conservative Fox News personality - had to break in on air and ask them to make it stop, in what I consider to be one of the rare displays of balance I've seen on Fox since the election began.

And it goes on and on. Fox News dived all over a story from Insight, the online internet publication owned by the Washington Post, that reported that Senator Obama had attended a *madrasah* in Indonesia as a child, a type of school where young Muslim extremists are educated. They later had to broadcast 'clarifications' regarding the story, which was of course false, but have yet to do a complete 180 on the essence of the story's message.

We've had Liz Trotter, another Fox news reporter, crack a joke about assassinating Obama, graphics displayed during news stories referring to Michelle Obama as Barack's 'baby mama', and a host of other reporting that has begun to make Fox News look like they've lost their collective minds. But nothing, and I mean NOTHING tops Sean Hannity's lunatic ramblings night after night, after miserable night, over what he sees as Senator Obama's radicalism, evidenced of course by his association to the Reverend Jeremiah Wright.

Hannity's blatant attempts at keeping the Trinity United Church of Christ and a handful of comments made by its former pastor over the span of 30 years alive and well in the minds of Americans is also racist, pure and simple. Racism after all, has been defined as an intolerance of another race or other races, and what Sean Hannity has displayed in his constant, never-ending reporting about Senator Obama, Reverend Wright, Michelle Obama (and her lack of pride in her country), etc., etc. is precisely that - intolerance. Intolerance of the black experience, intolerance of a man's right to choose how and where he worships, intolerance of ideas different than his own - intolerance.

The idea that in a 2008 America, there are still people who don't understand that many in the black community are still vocal about the ravages of economic and social inequality that have weighed our collective progress down since slavery is amazing to me. And that a man as intelligent, as thought-provoking and learned as I thought Sean Hannity was can't seem to get past his flag-waving, love-me-or-leave-me American ideas long enough to acknowledge same is, well, disheartening.

And this, I think has been the most disappointing aspect of Fox News' post-racial melt down, because as I said before, I never thought of Sean Hannity as a racist before - just a staunchly conservative, opinionated personality.

Only those who refuse to acknowledge the differences in who we are as black people, and what our experiences in this country have been would listen to his ranting and hear anything other than crap. And yet, with the launching of his 'Stop Radical Obama Express', he's turned up the dial on the fear-mongering, race-baiting, and plain old lies all in order to quell the tide of support for a man who has never displayed even an ounce of intolerance for those different than himself in the twenty-plus years he has been a public servant. Mr. Hannity questions the judgment of Senator Obama over his association with Reverend Wright, but not John McCain's over his involvement in the Keating 5 scandals of the late-eighties. He berates Michelle Obama over the idea that this campaign has made her proud of her country for the first time in her life, but gives Cindy

McCain a total pass on her past drug addiction and theft, and she and her father's role in the same Keating scandals. And most disturbingly, he continues to drive home the idea that Senator Barack Obama is too 'radical' to be President, citing his ties to this controversial figure or that one, never bothering to expend a moment of airtime exploring the violent flip-flopping and pandering that John McCain has had to do in order to get and stay in the good graces of the Republican conservative wing.

But I guess he wouldn't, would he? Because then he WOULD be fair and balanced. I don't think that any of us that have set our sights on the transgressions of the Fox News Network want special treatment for Senator Obama or anyone else. I think we'd like for them to a) really try and be more responsible in their reporting, and b) take a deep and somber look at the level of bias they've introduced into this election cycle and put the brakes on it. It does nothing but harm the process, and I believe that most honest, good-hearted Americans are not buying it anyway.

If that weren't true, Senator Obama would not be smoking John McCain in the polls in so many important swing states, as he is as of this writing. Sean, you are a brilliant guy - can't you and your buddies at the network find a way to fight this battle based on the issues and not the fears of the American people? I hope you can, because BWFO is watching you, dude, all of you, and we're going to shoot the tires off of the "Stop Radical Obama Express". Believe that.

With a Supporter Like Jesse....

Oh boy.

Are you like me? When you saw the video today of Jesse
Jackson whispering to an unknown guest about cutting
off Senator Obama's family jewels on FOX NEWS no
less, did you cringe? Did you pray for a meteor or
asteroid (I've never known the difference) to fall from
the sky and incinerate Reverend Rude in an instant and
in such a way that it would leave everything and
everyone who might be around him intact and
unharmed?

A better question - when you heard that self-serving,
foul-mouthed, political call-boy say what could only be
described as "the dumbest crap I've ever heard, bar none"
with a look on his face like he'd just stolen the last Pop-
Tart and left the empty box in the pantry right before
dinner, did YOU read more into it than the media did?

I did. But first things first.

By now, unless you've been sleeping off a Twinkie binge, you know that Jesse Jackson, my favorite foot-in-mouther and yours, was caught yet a-(damned)-gain on tape, casting aspersions on our favorite Senator. I wish I could tell you that he accused Senator Obama of bad breath. I wish I could tell you that he had questioned, oh, Senator Obama's taste in neck ties. Heck, I even wish I could report to you that in a moment of misogyny, he lewdly declared Michelle Obama, "hot like lava". I wish I could tell you that he had said ANYTHING but what came out of his mouth when he thought he wasn't being heard. But hey - we ARE talking about Jesse Jackson here.

At some point during his interview with Fox Fake-News channel, Reverend (I REPEAT) REVEREND Jesse Jackson let the following words slip from his lips: (Viewer Discretion Is Advised):

"See, Barack been, um, talking down to black people. I wanna cut his nuts off."

My boy definitely gets the "WTF" award for this week. Listen, what he said was shocking, true. But WHAT he said was not nearly as shocking as HOW he said it. If you haven't seen the video, please take five and locate it on CNN and have a look. I'll wait.

218

Did you see what I saw?!?! There was an insidiousness to his remarks, and the devious way he let them slither out of his mouth just oozed, "Yeah - this dude thinks he's taken the love of my black people away from ME?!?! He thinks he can roll through and usurp my 'I-almost-became-president-even-though-I-never-really-got-close' legacy?!?!? Aw, naw, naw, he's actually been talkin' down to my people, so I'm 'bout to expose him for what he really is, thus restoring the faith and love of da black race to its rightful place - with me, with me, WITH MEEEEEEEE!!!"

Stop - don't close the browser! I'm being harsh, you say? I'm reading too much into Jesse's latest round of jaw jappin' you say? Uhhhhh, I don't think so. And here's why.

As you may recall, in a previous article, I wrote about my suspicions that Jesse Jackson's hesitance to back Barack Obama at the time was probably attributable to a pretty bad 'Hatorade' habit. My supposition was that Reverend Jackson, himself once a Presidential candidate of course, simply could not fathom the success of the young, popular upstart from Illinois, and similarly, could not resist (again, at the time) publicly dissing his efforts to win the Democratic nomination. Further, I hypothesized that Mr. Jackson would rather have done whatever he could to derail Senator Obama so that he could stand over his political carcass and cry, "See, he's JUST as black and unelectable as I am!!! See! Seeeeeeeeee!", than stand by the historic sidelines as someone who came outta nowhere, put together a stellar campaign organization, and by all accounts just did it all better, faster, and stronger than Jesse was able to.

And I'm sorry folks; I believe it to this day. Jesse *just can't stop hating on my boy.* So let's just revisit once again, PRECISELY what Reverend "Needs-To-Focus-On-Hatin-The-Game" had to say to the co-guest on Fox News who shall remain nameless:

"See, Barack been, um, talking down to black people. I wanna cut his nuts off."

Okay. Here's the real problem with this, people - I watched the video half a dozen times. Mr. Jackson has already started to call in his explanations to the media, saying that he was taken 'out of context', so I've been sitting here, squinting at the screen as I watch the video for the last half hour, turning my head from side to side, trying to do something, anything that would make me hear or see what he said in any other context than what he, well, meant to say it in. No luck.

The look on his face, the tone in his voice, the very way he delivered that *last* line - "I wanna cut his nuts off", did not say, "Man, I'm so MAD at Barack, I could just CUT HIS NUTS OFF!" No. It said, "I GOT this sucka now!"

Let that marinate. Feel free to go watch the video again and tell me what YOU see.

But here's the best part - I've also heard his apology, and while his contrition might seem convincing, his explanation of what he meant to convey is laughable. Reverend Jackson actually presumes to lecture Senator Obama on the need to deliver a 'broader, moral' message to black people, one that doesn't look down on them, but stresses urban justice, and pushes for policies that I guess will somehow magically make so many black men stop leaving their kids in single parent homes. This from a man who had to briefly withdraw from public life after it was discovered that he had not only, a) fathered a love child with a young hottie on his staff during an extra-marital affair, but b), used Rainbow Push Coalition money to fund a move for her, and to pay her for "consulting services". THIS man let the word 'moral' spring from his lips today.

Now, I realize that Jesse is no stranger to controversy, or to sticking his foot in his mouth, and that you might be thinking that I'm over-reacting somewhat. By I have to disagree - in an age where black women are heading up more households than ever before, and when 70% of OUR children are born out of wedlock, and when it seems more of our men go to prison than earn college degrees, some things needed to be said, and I support Senator Obama 100% in having the courage to say them.

But - I also acknowledge that some of Jesse's points have merit. A broader conversation DOES need to take place about the fact that in this country, a college-educated black man will still tend to be overlooked in favor of a

221

white man with none of his credentials by most corporate recruiters. And a broader conversation DOES need to occur about the fact that the residual effects of slavery are still being felt in our communities, even if just financially. And a broader conversation DOES need to take place about the self-loathing and doubt that often times derail our efforts to snatch our rightful chunk of the American Dream.

We need to have LOTS of conversations. But the FIRST one we need to have is about why one of our prolific black leaders would ever feel the need to cut anything off of Senator Obama or anyone else, literally or figuratively. There needs to be a discussion about the public faces, and the not-so public faces of the people that we trust to represent our interests, even informally. And there needs to be a discussion about how if we can't come together as a people to support one of our own, someone who is clearly so ready, so capable, so *destined* to lead this country, we cannot possibly hope to come together and have a meaningful dialog about how to begin to make a dent in the socio-economic condition of so many of our masses who have been left behind - that "broader, moral" discussion Reverend Jackson so passionately seeks.

That's IT, son. You just lost your civil rights leader card. You do NOT get to proclaim yourself a leader of black men, and then connive and scheme to derail the efforts of one of our beloved. The Obama train is headed to the future, Jesse - for some reason, you've chosen to hold onto the end of it, your heels digging into the dirt, sparks flying, trying to slow it down. What's worse? Today, Reverend Jackson, you proved that you'd even go so far as to pull the emergency brake on the train that so many of us are riding on, if given half a chance. And that sucks.

So, what us gon' do for a leader now, Black America? Hey! I know! I say we go with the man that has shown that he can lead ALL Americans, and conduct himself always in a way that we can respect and be proud of as Black Americans. It's been pretty sad to watch the shenanigans of some of the men who claim to have our best interests at heart during this process - Andrew Young, John Lewis (before he converted), Jesse. It's disheartening, but I guess we can take solace in the fact that even the dirtiest of dirt done in the dark always comes to light. Man, you think Jesse would have learned THAT lesson by now.

The Obama-Moses Ad: Or, PTTMCHLICMAM

PTTMCHLICMAM? We'll get to that in a moment.

First an acknowledgment:

It's getting increasingly harder to write these blog entries, primarily because there's so much to write about, it's difficult to settle on something and just, well, write it. But this morning, the McCain campaign has bestowed upon me an incredible gift - the gift of a lifted writer's block. Thank you, John McCain!

Okay (clear throat). So, if you're like me, you spent some part of yesterday scratching your head, trying to understand why the McCain campaign thinks that an ad depicting Moses (played by a recently deceased and beloved actor), and showing Senator Obama in various stages of his campaign (sometimes joking, sometimes lifting audiences with one of his soaring speeches) is anything but - dumb. And offensive if you REALLY loved "The Ten Commandments".

This new ad was just as strange and confusing as the now infamous "Britney-Paris' advertisement. The truth is, it was only because I had been forewarned that the BP ad was out there that I even knew it *was* a McCain ad. The references to Britney Spears and Paris Hilton were strange to be sure, but the ad, like this new one, shows our favorite Senator in front of adoring crowds, and has a constant 'Obama! Obama!' chant in the background. If you're watching these ads and you're a supporter of Senator Obama's, you won't know whether to cheer or collapse on the floor in a fit of confusion. But I can tell you that what I was at NO time tempted to do, was doubt the importance of Senator Obama's ability to inspire, because (and please listen closely Mr. McCain) *that is what real leaders do.*

I think the McCain-inites have stepped in it this time. If I were writing ads for the Obama Campaign, I would be all over this like a cheap suit, because in attempting to question whether or not Senator Obama can lead, what they've *really* done is shined a light on the fact that as one who has an almost endless ability to inspire, he possesses what is considered to be one of the most important traits of a truly great leader.

That's Management 101 people. Any random Google search of 'What makes a great leader?' will return a list similar to the one below:

225

1. Visionary
2. **Inspirational**
3. Strategic
4. Tactical
5. Focused
6. Persuasive
7. Likable
8. Decisive
9. Ethical
10. Open to criticism

Let's examine, shall we? Let's see - John McCain is no visionary, and I think that by producing these ads his campaign has all but admitted that he's about as inspirational as a bag of dirt. His ability to act strategically and tactically? Hmmm - he's been in the Senate for like, a billion years, so I guess one has to assume that he has some measure of these skills. Let's keep it moving.

Watching him on the campaign trail, I haven't seen much focus, and let's face it; he is neither persuasive nor likable. I'm sure he's plenty decisive, but he's proven in the past that ethics could be a problem for him. And finally, if you've seen him growl at one of his press corps reporters from time to time, you know he's not the best at taking criticism. The evidence is overwhelming - the McCain campaign *really* needs to stop asking whether or not Senator Obama can lead, before someone turns the question back around on them.

This is a slippery slope for a number of reasons. The McCain campaign has to know that any line of attack that assumes that Senator Obama is all glorious speeches and no substance is a direct insult to me and people like me - and Senator Obama has said as much in his responses to these strange ads. And I feel it personally, because by throwing up the whole 'Obama thinks he's Moses' thing, the McCain campaign is accusing me, and all of you, of being Pied-Piper like lemmings, with no real discernible ability to choose a candidate based on the issues, especially if he happens to be charismatic, drop dead gorgeous, and an impassioned and eloquent speaker.

Following that line of thought, there are a lot of great leaders who should have had ad campaigns levied at them chocked full of mocking references to biblical figures. Try to imagine what it would have been like if in 1980, Jimmy Carter's campaign, desperate to stem the tide of admiration for Ronald Reagan and his good looks, articulate speeches, and Washington outsider status, had resorted to such tactics, perhaps by producing ads comparing him to Jonah, complete with a big whale that spewed peanuts, or hair gel.

The hair gel thing was a reference to Ronald Reagan's always perfectly coiffed hair. I'll move on.

Or if in 1960, Richard Nixon, upset by a clear upstaging from a young and attractive John F. Kennedy Jr., had somehow been able to foist ads upon us that compared him to John The Baptist - can't you just see it? John The Baptist baptizing Uncle Sam in some lame attempt at belittling JFK?

Sounds ridiculous, I know, but no more so than the crap the McCain campaign put out this past week. Sadly, though their methods are goofy, I actually would have been disappointed if they hadn't come back with *something* after having to sit through footage of Senator Obama in front of 200,000 chanting Europeans last week, all of whom seemed to be screaming, "We want you to lead the Free World, and not the old guy! We want you to lead the Free World and not the old guuuuuuyyyyyy!" That would send any candidate over the edge. But it simply points out McCain's clear disadvantage to produce these kinds of ads, and does nothing to change the inescapable fact that inspiration is what we want in our leaders. And those of us who know, know that Senator Obama is the near perfect combination of inspiration, brilliance and charisma. And more importantly than that, he knows how to inspire people to *action*, and then lead them when they move to act. John McCain couldn't inspire me to even turn up the volume on one of his speeches, let alone do anything else he asked of me.

I understand this is all just politics. I do. But what I don't get is how the McCain campaign could possibly get away with a line of attack that is first of all offensive, secondly - more than a little ridiculous, and thirdly, borderline blasphemy. Attacking Senator Obama because he's inspirational? That's like blasting Kobe Bryant because he's good at popping 3-pointers.

If the McCain campaign wants to go all 'can he lead?' on us, then let us examine the facts, lest we forget:

Senator Obama has led a campaign that on its own, and without special interest PAC money, that as of this writing has raised over $340,000,000 dollars.

Senator Obama has single-handedly awakened the American people from a long, tortuous slumber, brought on by decade after decade of exclusionary politics, and moved millions of them to get and stay involved in the political process.

Senator Obama has run an organization that at every step of the way has been professional, productive, organized, and meticulous in its dealings with his opponents, the media, and each other.

Senator Obama has consistently stayed on the defensive when it comes to negative campaigning, and has at no time resorted to the childish and misleading tactics that the McCain campaign has this week, and has been adamant about keeping his message about the issues and the needs of the American people.

Yikes - I could go on and on. But the bottom line is, I was not fooled by the McCain campaign's attempt to lessen the importance of the man who is destined to become the next President of the United States, and I don't think very many other people will be either. Just check out the blogs, they're telling the story this morning. I think even McCain supporters are wincing over this one, and it's hard to blame them. By now, they too are convinced as I am that this is 'PTTMCHLICMAM' - Proof-That-The-McCain-Campaign-Has-Lost-It's-Collective-Monkey-Ass-Mind.

Against All Odds: Denver Here I Come!

Amazing. About this time a little over a year and a half ago I was seated at this very computer, typing away at maybe my third or fourth blog post for Black Women for Obama. Since then of course, I've written dozens.

Back then, BWFO was just...a concept. An idea that I had that America needed to understand that there was a segment of the black community, in particular black women, who were squarely in Senator Obama's corner. At the time, I wasn't aware of any *specific* black women who were Obama supporters other than me, but I was certain they were out there.

See, I had just finished reading 'The Audacity of Hope', and I was a changed person. After reading Senator Obama's brilliant narrative on America, our politics, and our place in the world, I knew that as an intelligent, engaged writer, mother, and educator, I had to get involved in helping to bring about the vision that Senator

Obama outlined in his book. I believed it then, and I still believe it now.

A lot has happened since then. Since then, my mother has been diagnosed with breast cancer, and undergone a radical double mastectomy. Since then, I've been laid off from a job that I loved, and found another one that I am blessed to have and equally fond of. Since then, I've been married, the economy has taken a violent down-turn, my son has started middle school, I've been elected a delegate from my district here in Georgia, and on and on and on. So many changes, some good and some bad. And through it all, my belief in Senator Obama and my commitment to his eventual Presidency has never wavered, not once.

Not that my involvement has been non-stop. Like many of you (I'm sure), there have been times when I simply could not find the time to do my Obama duty. At times, I simply couldn't find the energy, and at times I even had trouble mustering the will. But it was never because my faith in Senator Obama and his vision for our nation's future faltered; oh no. It was always because life, as it so often does, had thrown me some curve ball that caused me to have to temporarily take my eye off of the prize. But like a soldier wounded in combat, I am anxious to once again don my battle fatigues and re-join my battalion, and Denver is my opportunity to do so in grand fashion.

Ironically, my effort to raise the funds necessary to get to Denver turned out to be one of the most challenging obstacles of all. For weeks and weeks now, I have been singularly focused on finding a way to make it to Denver so that I can proudly cast my vote as an Obama delegate. And though nothing but death would have kept me from it, it was an uphill battle that I am not that anxious to repeat, even though I know it will be well worth it.

And so I'm poised now to board a plane to join the other delegates from Georgia's 7th Congressional District and the rest of the Georgia delegation in Denver to do my part to formalize Senator Obama's nomination, and the feeling is phenomenal. Against every obstacle that could possibly have been thrown at me, including a myriad of personal issues, several large boulder-sized financial road blocks, and what could only be described as a deep mental fatigue, I am preparing to head to Denver to do my part. Cast my vote. Wave my signs and wear any funny hats that come my way. And as I think about the experiences I have to look forward to next week, I realize that for the first time in my life, I know what a real privilege it is to be a part of the political process. To go beyond just showing up to vote in the general election to getting really and truly engaged from the start, and seeing it through to the end.

Bottom line is, we did it. Months and months of writing, and discussing, and meeting, and strategizing, and debating, and traveling, and phone calling, and bumper-stickering, and walking door-to-door have finally paid off, and we are just a few short days away from watching what so many thought was an impossibility. For me, it has been so completely gratifying that it defies description. Knowing from where Senator Obama came at the beginning of this process, knowing that he is about to take his permanent place in history is exciting, and truly amazing. Please know that as I take my place with my delegation, and cast my official vote to nominate Senator Obama for President, I will be thinking of and representing all of you, the strong and faithful Obama supporters from all over the country who could not be dissuaded and would not be denied. Congratulations goes out to all of you - I think it's safe to speak for Senator Obama to say that he could not have done it without you. Without us.

So Denver, here I come. Ready to help put the cherry on top of what has been an illuminating election season. And once the convention's over, it will be time for me and all of you to find that last rush of adrenaline, that final burst of energy that we're going to need to drive it home for Senator Obama in November. Nothing else but complete victory will do. Let's get this thing done in Denver, and then close the chapter on the Bush policy years for once and for all.

On Community Organizing

The Republican Convention has been nothing if not entertaining. I started to skip the whole thing - I thought it would just be too darned hard to watch so many uppity people casting aspersions on my favorite Senator and yours. But I tuned in, and after three nights of truth-bending rhetoric, name calling and selective memory recall from the Republican smash machine, I'm alright. I'm just fine.

It was yesterday, during Sarah Palin's speech that a deep calm came over me. Somewhere around the time when Ms. Palin began to mock Senator Obama's background in community organizing. It was then, right then, that I realized that these people either a) have no idea what they're up against, or b) can't admit it to themselves. Either way, I'm golden.

Of what do I speak you ask? Well, you heard it - the notion put right out there for the world to see and hear by none other than the unqualified-one herself, Sarah

Palin, that Senator Obama's work as a community organizer consisted of no 'actual responsibilities'. Which is to say (I guess) that his skills as an organizer have also had no impact on the campaign, or will hold no relevance for his presidency. That's funny to me. Is it funny to you?

If it isn't it should be. Way back when, during the days leading up to the hotly contested Texas primary, I found myself in Austin, Texas in a high-rise building phone-banking with total strangers, when Ashley Collier, one of the Obama campaign's field directors walked up to me and exclaimed excitedly, "Miss Pat, is that you?!?" I had worked with Ashley and many of the other campaign workers in the Atlanta office during the Georgia primary run up. I had helped plan events, held phone-banking nights at the campaign office, etc., and so I had gotten to know Ashley pretty well.

Space was at a premium in the suite of offices that was the epicenter of Obama campaign activity in Austin. I had had to battle it out with retirees and college students for desk space to spread out the call sheets that I was working from each day. To my delight, Ashley advised me that she shared a small cramped office with two other campaign employees who happened to be out of the office on that particular day, and that she would be happy to let me crash with her to do my work while I was there. I was thrilled - it made me feel like a campaign insider!

I'll never forget the time I spent with Ashley there that day. We talked about her work on the campaign, the crazy 'Texas Two-Step', her thoughts about Obama's chances, and the impassioned men and women that made up the volunteer corps of the campaign. We talked about the success of Camp Obama, and I mentioned to her how tight a ship the campaign leadership seemed to run. And that's when she said it - that's when she said the words that made me realize, really for the first time, the true genius of the man for which I had worked so hard.

"(Paraphrasing) Oh, this is all Barack. He's running every bit of this campaign - he is a brilliant *organizer*".

A brilliant organizer. *A brilliant organizer.* I've never forgotten those words, and knowing what I know now about how Senator Obama has been able to inspire millions of apathetic Americans to get off their butts and get engaged, how he's amassed more money for his campaign through individual donations than any politician in history, how he's given birth to a new generation of activists and taught them not only how to get and stay involved, but how to organize to get others involved as well? I can't do anything BUT laugh at the idea that Republicans would belittle his community organizing skills, since it's the ultimate organized community that is poised to help him kick John McCain's butt in November.

Yep. I'm truly gratified. Because, though it is not easy to turn from the train wreck, watching night after night, wanting to look away, but being somehow unable to, I have heard nothing, and I mean NOTHING that could possibly be mistaken as truth, and I know what millions and millions around the country and the world like me know - this is Senator Obama's time, and no amount of name calling, belittling, or posturing from a chorus of Republican loud-mouths will change that.

And so, little Miss Firearms, go ahead and mock Senator Obama's community organizing past. While you and your buddies shoot moose and swill beer and have a great laugh, Senator Obama's organized community will continue to do the work that will push us across the historic finish line to a new direction for this country, and a total rejection of the last eight years of damaging, deceptive, destructive, and divisive Bush policies. Let 'em say what they want - I'm PROUD to be a part of the organized Obama community, and proud of every bit of the journey that has brought Senator Barack Obama to the edge of history - including those days in Chicago long ago.

Race in the Race

It's been a roller coaster ride. For those of us who have been Obama supporters from Day One, it's been like being on the world's largest roller coaster after eating a chili dog from Atlanta's famed Varsity Restaurant. It's actually even worse.

First - we endured the looks of confusion on the faces of our friends and family, when we told them we were going to a meeting of Barack Obama volunteers. "Barack what?" was the most frequent response to such a pronouncement. A brief explanation of who Barack Obama was back then, almost always elicited the same response. "Girl, you crazy. This country not gon' vote fa no black man."

I can remember it like it was yesterday. Even my 77 year-old mother, turning up her nose at me in disgust over what she perceived as my colossal waste of time - the meetings, the phone calls, the organizing. She accused me of caring more about "that Borock O-bama" than I did her, my house, or my son. Or even my job. And yes, she was sure, with everything in her, that he had no chance of winning the nomination. No chance at all.

But the early supporters endured, all the way through Super Tuesday, when the people of Iowa, most of them white Americans sent a lightning bolt through the country by casting their ballots mostly for the junior Senator from Illinois. The news was a-buzz with the historic nature of what was perceived at the time as a Clinton upset, and everything began to change. Some of my brothers and sisters, my friends and family began to actually ask themselves, "Could it really happen?"

But consequently, all manner of new ludicrousness began:

"The Clintons have always been there for black people - what do we know about this dude?"

"He's not black enough - he don't care about our issues!"

"A vote for him is a wasted vote!"

"He need to change his name if he wants to even have a chance!"

And my personal favorite…"I can't vote for that man, they might assassinate him!"

Black people were running into each other emotionally - we didn't know what to feel or what was coming next. And then the Obama campaign machine proved to us all that not only could he win the primary - he also had a chance - some chance, of winning the election.

How did they do it? In part, by almost completely playing down Senator Obama's race, and instead opting to highlight his skills as a uniter and change agent. He wowed us all black, white and brown, with his ability to help us see what was possible, and gave us all a reason to feel a hope that was so strong, that by the time the Reverend Jeremiah Wright flap reached its climax, we had begun to believe that Senator Obama was uniquely qualified to help begin truly turning the battleship of racial bigotry in this country. It seemed that he might even have had what it took to help the white majority in this country better understand the black condition; why for some, an anger still boils just below the surface, as he did in his now historic speech from Philadelphia. And though it was a rough and rocky road, he made it through and we began to believe even more.

Then, of course, he fought hard and long to make it across the finish line to clinch the nomination. And before I knew it, all the naysayers were loudly celebrating, and proclaiming their disbelief over his accomplishment, and daring to believe that this country truly had crossed an important milestone. It was time to look ahead to the General Election, and so many of us had hope in our hearts, and a renewed belief in the progress we'd made as a nation.

More money raised than any campaign in history. A trip abroad that proved he is loved and admired by citizens of other nations in a way that is unprecedented in American politics. And an acceptance speech, given in Denver's Invesco Field, to over 84,000 supporters, all crowning achievements for a campaign that has been almost flawlessly executed, and that also by the way, stopped one of the most prolific political machines of our time dead in its tracks.

And now that we are several weeks into the General Election, a daunting question is again beginning to take center stage amongst the pundits and nightly news media. A question that given the dire nature of our economy, the general distaste for the human and monetary costs of the war in Iraq, the record number of foreclosures, and the general and overriding belief that the nation is heading in the wrong direction, begs for an answer - is race the reason why Senator Obama is not at least 20 points ahead of John McCain in the polls?

I was at Invesco field when Senator Obama gave what was by all accounts an incredible speech. On the way out, as I followed the throng of people exiting the arena, I overheard a conversation between two white gentlemen, who, after being suitably impressed by his speech and the flawless execution of the whole night, wondered aloud about the same thing:

"Man, that speech was amazing. That crowd was amazing. I don't understand why we're not up by 20 or 30 points in the polls", said the first gentleman.

"It's his race, pure and simple", said the second. "It's hard to believe, but there are still a lot of people out there that just won't vote for a black man."

I could feel tears well up in my eyes. Because it dawned on me at that moment that despite the crowds, despite the miraculous fund-raising, the inspirational and sometimes brilliantly instructional speeches - it might still in the end, come down to how many people in this country can set aside their irrational prejudices in order to do what's best for the nation. There are no two ways about it - the shockingly low difference in the candidates' poll numbers in my opinion, bears this out.

It reminds me of one of the most amazing, and yet most chilling movies I've ever seen - "A Time To Kill". In it, Samuel L. Jackson, the father of a young girl, has to stand trial for murdering two white men who had brutally beat and raped his daughter, and left her for dead at the bottom of a lake. By some miracle, the girl was found and saved, but her womb had been destroyed, and she bore outward physical scars, and internal scars that would never go away.

Despite the brutal nature of the crime, Jackson's character was treated like a vigilante, an angry black man bent on exacting justice against the perpetrators of the horrible crime against his daughter; the white inhabitants of the small town gave hardly a thought to what the little girl had gone through, and wanted Samuel L. to fry for murdering the men who were clearly guilty, and clearly unrepentant. The anguish he must have felt at the thought of what was done to his daughter; the insanity it must have induced never entered most of the town's minds. Enter Matthew McConaughey.

Matthew McConaughey was Samuel L's defense attorney. Faced with a jury of all whites, from a southern town where racial disharmony was the norm, and working for a defendant who had in fact murdered the two men in question, the odds were against him and Samuel L. And it looked like it was all but over until he did something extraordinary.

If you saw the movie, you know what he did. He stepped up before the jury, and asked them to use their imaginations to envision the little black girl, as he told the anguished story of what she had endured at the hands of the perpetrators. He described every blow, every atrocity in graphic enough detail to paint a vivid, disturbing picture. And at the end of it all, he asked the jury to picture it, really picture it all - and then imagine that the girl was white.

I'm overcome by the need to do the same thing to the American people. I want to get a bull horn that will reach the rural areas of Pennsylvania, and Ohio, and the farms of Missouri. I want to implore them to imagine a man, who was a genius student, a graduate of Columbia University, who would go on to Harvard, graduate at the top of his class, become the president of the Harvard Law Review. Imagine that that man went on to become a constitutional scholar, and lecturer, and that rather than take the lucrative road to wealth and financial comfort for his family, chose instead to give himself over to a life of service as first an Illinois State Senator, and then a United States Senator. Imagine that this man, through his unique vision for the country, had inspired so many people, that he was literally called to service, and drafted to run for President of the United States. I want ALL of white America to picture it, really picture it all.

And then imagine that he's black.

Sarah Palin, or "The Bad Re-Make of Pretty Woman"

Ok. Seriously. I was just sitting here on my lumpy couch, minding my own business, getting my steady diet of news about the election, when I saw something that convinced me that either a) I have a brain tumor, or b) someone has punched a hole in the space time continuum. Or both.

Today, at a town-hall-style rally with Wisconsin voters, Sarah Palin, the least vetted candidate for high public office in all of history, suggested yet again, that Americans need to get to know the 'real' Barack Obama, and that because of his nefarious associations - and this is when I think I felt my brain tumor twitch - Barack Obama would 'diminish the prestige of the presidency'.

For real, Sarah?

It's hard to even know where to begin. Matt Damon suggested that this all seemed like a bad Disney movie,

246

but if you ask me, it's starting to feel more like a bad re-make of 'Pretty Woman'.

Let me just ask you this - just this ONE question. Would the American electorate have to endure this crap if John McCain had plucked an over-weight, bespectacled white woman out of obscurity, lined her up on stage next to him with her pregnant daughter and newly cleaned-up beau after being unable to prove that he had vetted her in any meaningful way? Would we be forced to suspend disbelief about, oh, experience, and relevance of education to the V.P. job if Sarah Palin herself were in fact a fat, dumpy, pimply-faced woman, who had gone to 5 different colleges before finally managing to squeak out a degree in Journalism (a profession which she would go on to flame out in before running for Mayor of a town with a population smaller than some college graduating classes)? And if this less than attractive woman was partial to shooting forest creatures out of a helicopter and being prayed for by witch-hunting evangelical extremists, I dunno - do you think the situation would be just an itty-bitty bit different?

You betcha, there. My friends to the right of the political spectrum can say what they will - Sarah Palin has mesmerized these otherwise mostly rational Americans who call themselves Conservatives not with her staunch right-wing beliefs or glowing readiness for high office, but literally with a wink and a smile. And she's done so while being coddled like Julia Roberts in *Pretty Woman*, one of the most irritating moves of all time, being spirited away whenever a real journalist or even a college student gets too close to asking her a substantive question. And yet, there she was today, standing before yet another adoring crowd actually asking the question with a straight face - when are Americans going to get the answers they need about Barack Obama?

Man, Sarah - for real?

I have all the answers I need about Barack Obama, Sarah-poo. He's been deflecting upper cuts and body blows from the media for going on two years now. No, I'm good on Barack. I am however, like many other *sane* Americans, still curious about a couple of things where *you're* concerned, my friend.

Like the whole 'Trooper-gate' saga. Of course, since you've refused to answer questions about that, I guess I'm what you'd call 'outta luck, there'.

Okay - well, how about that 'bridge to friggin' nowhere, thing?' I'd like a couple of answers about why you claimed to oppose it when you were photographed wearing a t-shirt saying that you supported it? Any answers on that one? No, I guess not.

Well shucks, let's see. How about that snarly Alaskan Secessionist thing - can I at least get a dead-pan denial about that? Hmmmm, crickets on that one as well. Well gosh, darn it!

Alright, missy - what I'd *really* like to know is why you're not answering the tough questions that are being posed of Senators Obama and Biden on a daily basis. Heck, even Senator McCain for that matter. It's the very fact that you, who has been more sequestered from the media than any candidate for the vice presidency that I can personally recall, would actually stand up before crowds of your admirers and demand answers from Senator Obama, that I'm convinced that we all now live in a world where up has become down. And the beautiful can get away with anything.

Let's face it - I am a heterosexual woman, and even *I* know that Sarah Palin is gorgeous. It's creepy. It is after all, part of our human nature to be drawn towards those things that we perceive as visually appealing, I get that. But to hear the endless drivel, the consistently non-sensical, cataclysmically sophomoric retorts come spewing from Sarah Palin day after day, in some way creates this weird dichotomy of reactions, where you can't help but think she's cute, even as you wretch over what you're hearing.

The whole thing has taken on air of surreal-ness that I can't WAIT to see end. Her candidacy, and any gains she has made for the Republican ticket is nothing but a reminder that even with something this important, there are those of us who will always be slaves to our baser selves.

So Sarah - I ain't made atcha. Lucky for America, your presence is a temporary one, and after November 4th, only the wild animals of Alaska will need fear 'ya. But until that time, I'd give anything, a lung, a right arm, anything, if you would stop with the Jedi mind tricks - you came along a little late, dear. This country has gotten to know Barack Obama VERY well, which is why he is in the position that he's in right now, and you're in the unenviable position of playing attack dog for a man who himself is being dogged by his unpopular policies and a series of gaffes, missteps, and straight up blunders that rival any in modern American politics. But hey - you really are gosh darn pretty!

On Obama and Black Boys

As of this writing, the current national Gallup poll has
Senator Obama leading by a respectable percentage;
several previously red states are either leaning or solidly
in the Obama column, and Senator McCain is fighting
tooth and nail to hold on to other Republican strong
holds, including his own home state of Arizona. Though
most of us are afraid to say so, it appears that we are in
fact about to see our collective dreams come true - one
that many of us thought could not happen, and definitely
not in our lifetimes. We are mere days away from what
could be one of the most historic and defining moments
in this nation's history, and as a black woman, it's been
hard for me to know where to begin when it comes to
expressing my thoughts about what's coming.

There are so many black women out there who, like me,
are raising young black men. Due to a recent marriage,
I'm now raising three. And it is as much a sign of how
much this nation has changed that in some ways, my
three sons are oblivious to the importance of the coming

event, as it is an indictment on our society that as women raising black men, we've longed for someone, anyone to ease our fears about our sons' futures and to be the role models that our young boys have so desperately needed for so long. Not that we haven't had strong models for them *at all*, but we've been hard pressed to find them outside the fields of sports, music, or other areas of the entertainment industry.

I was left alone to raise the only child I've ever given birth to when I was just four months pregnant. The pain and fear I felt at the time soon gave way to resentment, and then to hatred so pronounced that it threatened to swallow me whole. I had tried my best to play by the rules, only becoming pregnant after six years of marriage during which I had begun to think that I was incapable of having a child.

The news of my pregnancy was at once joyous and terrifying, as it became increasingly apparent that I would be forced to raise my son alone. Back then, I could not comprehend how it was that the father of my only child could not understand how much his son needed him, how much I needed him, and the pain of the rejection of me and my son was unbearable at times. It was everything I could do after the birth of my sweet David to will myself on a daily basis to be grateful for the part-time status of his father, and the modest child support he paid faithfully each month. But it was what I had to do, for my son's sake, and also because a guiding hand, a role-model, a mentor, my son's father could and would never be.

What was even harder is that it wasn't long before I realized that I had to find some way to learn to forgive my ex-husband; I eventually realized that he himself was and is a product of a shattered home, and ill-equipped to play the role of father and husband. Raised without his birth father, and ultimately without his birth mother, he had no real guiding hand, no role model of his own to speak of. He was clothed and fed, and taken care of in very basic ways only; as a result, he had no foundation given to him in what it meant to be a father and a husband, to raise a black boy in this society, or to set and achieve goals of any kind. In his life, he has been played only whatever hand he has been dealt, and the result is that though he loves our son as much as he knows how to, he has nothing meaningful in the way of mentorship to give him.

My story is not unique. From the young woman who may have gotten caught after a bad lapse in judgment, to those who like me, watched their husbands walk out on them after years of marriage, literally leaving them holding a blue diaper bag, many black women have had to come to terms with the idea that we have been left alone to raise little men. As a population, we have allowed ourselves to fall into a cycle of family disintegration that has become all too common place. These days, it's the African-American kids who *live* in in-tact two parent homes who are the weird ones. In our communities, having a father who is in the home, productive and engaged has become a novelty. A tragic, gut-wrenching novelty.

But for the most part as black women, we've persevered. Doing all that we can to expose our sons to the right influences, to talk tough to them when we need to in their fathers' absence, and to do and say whatever we can to try to mold them into the men they need to be. Sometimes without the benefit of having had a male role model to emulate ourselves, and all the while praying that OUR sons will prove wrong the ugly statistics that we can't escape or get out of our heads.

The reality is, the problem is generational, and has its roots in slavery and the systemic destruction of the African family unit as it was when slaves were brought to this country. Many stories of the time tell of how upon arriving on these shores, men were immediately separated from their children and wives, in order to begin the process of degradation and humiliation that would ensure that their spirits would be broken, and that they would willingly comply with their masters' wishes. It began way back then, and in some form persists to this day because of our inability to re-discover our strong family ties, through the lingering effects of Jim Crow, the confusion of first segregation and then forced desegregation, and the plain old racism and failed attempts at evening the playing field (like welfare, and in some respects affirmative action).

So it was, that we the black mothers of America found ourselves; over the years, frightened beyond all measure that our young men would be sacrificed to the ravages of an unfair justice system, or worse to the violence of the mean streets; or engulfed in the culture of fake opulence and self-degradation that is some rap music, and some aspects of the Hip-Hop culture; or lost and forgotten in an educational system that is tilted towards their white counterparts, and none too anxious to fix itself in order to help to turn the tide of drop-outs and illiterate graduates it produces in startling higher proportions in the minority community. And most of all we were certainly convinced that though blacks in this country have made many strides, there were still some very obvious limits, when on the national stage walked Barack Obama.

Now please don't get me wrong. I know that Senator Obama is not the second coming, or even the answer to all our problems, but what he has become is a shining beacon of hope, and proof of what we've all known all along - that black men can be real fathers, good husbands, and strong and thoughtful leaders. That in our communities, there is an untold number of little budding Barack Obama's waiting to happen. That with the proper care and feeding, our boys are capable of achieving the unthinkable. The beauty of Senator Obama is that he is not only a model as a legislator and candidate, he is *more so* as a father to his gorgeous daughters and husband to his wife.

And so, Senator Obama, along with all the other weight he carries on his shoulders, literally is carrying the hopes of the black boys who will soon be men in this country, who generation after generation, have been able to hide their brilliance and potential behind the mantle of racism that spawned the hopelessness that said that they could only ever go so far, or achieve so much. And he and his family stand as the most shining example of a strong family, black, white, or purple that we've seen on the national forefront in a long time. It is an astounding feeling, as the final days of the campaign fade away, to look forward to the days after November 4th, when we can all breathe an endless sigh of relief and spend our days reminiscing about the fight. And it will not be lost on any of us what this historic event can and will mean to the young black boys of this country, who after that date, will be able to say with confidence and without hesitation, "one day, I want to be President of the United States".

I get great joy in the wide-eyed wonder on my sons' faces when I tell them that once black kids and white kids couldn't play together - not totally unlike the giggle I get out of watching them collapse into a fit of laughter when I tell them that when I was their age, we only had four channels to watch on television. One day, my sons, will be able to astound *their* grandchildren with wild tales of a time in our nation's history when the idea of a black man running for President was laughable - unheard of. And hopefully, they will smile, and take great joy in their chuckles, and marvel at the innocence that comes from being the beneficiaries of the brave and remarkable accomplishments of those who came before us.

Celebration

It happened before we knew it. At precisely 11:00 pm Eastern Standard time, on November 4th, 2008, when we expected to begin hearing more state projections, all of the network and cable news outlets declared Senator Barack Obama to be the President-Elect of the United States of America.

I didn't do what I thought I would do. I was all prepared to collapse into a fit of tears, to become overwhelmed by the enormity of it all; to feel a huge release from the nervous tension that had been building for the last several days. Instead, what I felt was serenity, a peace that I couldn't explain. As my family and friends clapped and cheered and cried, I sat to myself, shaking my head at the idea that it could all be over just like that.

There is much to wonder about in what took place that night. What happened to the "Bradley Effect", or the voters (it was feared) who'd lied to pollsters about voting for Obama and then didn't? Where was the total desertion of "un-decideds" to the McCain camp that had been predicted by some? It was amazing – there were no states so close to call that the race would linger on for days or weeks. No long lines at the polls, or riots, or voter suppression to speak of, nothing. Just an awe-inspiringly decisive win on the part of President-Elect Obama, including in states that had not voted for a Democrat in several decades.

Even the highly-paid news pundits didn't know what had hit them. For days and weeks ahead of time, fears regarding the dreaded "Bradley Effect" had been the main topic of many of their shows, and going into election night, it was the one thing that no one was really sure about. I had long ago taken solace in the fact that if the Bradley Effect *was* in fact a real phenomenon, it would not necessarily be so after 26 years. I was confident, as was Michelle Obama that any such effect would have shown itself in the Primary.

And what of the un-decideds and the ever-tightening race the media warned us about up until the very last moment? CNN's before and after poll-of-polls results showed that even though some races absolutely *did* tighten at the end, the polls going into election night proved to be dead-on, primarily because un-decided voters essentially split down the middle in their support of the two candidates.

What about the long, oppressive lines at the polls? The voter suppression fears? Early voting made mince meat of these, in states where early voting was allowed, and in other states, lower than anticipated turn-out helped with the rest. Though it is inconceivable to me that anyone in this country who was eligible would not have been electrified into action by the excitement of this race, the truth is, more Democrats than ever turned out to vote, while fewer Republicans cast votes for *their* party than in 2004, an obvious reflection of the disparity in excitement levels between the two camps. A concerted effort on the part of both campaigns to monitor the polls for voter suppression and other problems apparently calmed the waters there.

The real truth of the matter is that Election Night 2008 was a brilliant culmination of an almost flawlessly executed campaign on the part of President-Elect Obama and his campaign strategists. We were knee deep in the primary season when I got a taste of how professional and well-run his organization was as a volunteer, and it never missed a beat. It helped as well to have a candidate with the mind and heart to win over Americans from all backgrounds, and untold people from every nation around the world, and whose message of hope and change gave most of us exactly what we needed to hear in some pretty turbulent times. One of the most beautiful things about the celebration that went into the night that night was that it literally took place in concert *all around the world* – even the staunchest Republican had to have been moved by the sight of the global euphoria, especially from the residents of Kenya, the land of Barack's father's birth.

As a black woman, it has been almost surreal, watching the nation suddenly become fixated on Michelle, Sasha and Malia Obama; already so much change, in a country where the disappearance of a small black child or an African-American woman has in the past, garnered almost no national media attention, especially as compared to our white counterparts. Suddenly, what Michelle Obama is wearing is the talk of the fashion world, and where she will send her daughters to school is on the minds of pundits and prognosticators the world over. Everything is changing right before our eyes, and it is a privilege to be able to see it all unfold.

All that is left now is for us to keep up the fight for a truly United States. Electing our first African-American President comes with great responsibility for the black men, women and children in this country. It is *not* okay to joke about making white people slaves; it is not okay to gloat over Obama's victory to even our *close* white friends, because he was not elected by blacks alone. It *is,* however, the time that we have been waiting for since the beginning of our history in this nation. We can officially close the chapter on systemic racism at the highest levels of government, and focus our efforts on the day to day problems of inequality that still plague our workplaces, schools, communities, and homes.

And we can begin to *be* the change we need. What would it *mean* for this country if the legions of Obama and McCain volunteers for that matter, black, white, and brown, were as determined to see that all of our children get a good education as they were that their candidate get elected? What would it mean for us all if that same army of volunteers assisted the elderly, helped feed the sick, aided veterans, and victims of natural disasters?

It would give an already enormously historic event new and lasting meaning. It would usher in a new era of true bi-partisanship and collective support that could get this country back on the road to being the one we once knew, after eight-years of mayhem. In other words, it would be what some of us fought so hard and long for - the kind of change that President-Elect Obama taught us to believe in.

Four Years Later: Are You In?

Are you in? It's the current battle cry of the 2012 version of the Obama Campaign, and though on its surface, it almost feels like a casual question, it's rife with much deeper meaning almost three-and-a-half years after the historic election of President Barack Obama.

On its face, and in basic terms, the question says *will you volunteer for me again? Will you donate regularly and at the historic levels you did in 2008?* But deep down, it forces those of us who worked so hard to support then Senator Obama to ask ourselves, *do we still believe in the vision and the man? Can we see Barack Obama's presidency in its totality and conclude that it has overall been a success, and that his policies and leadership have been better for the country?* Despite the historic nature of the election, and the joy we felt as African Americans – *has he delivered on the vision of America that he convinced so many of us was possible?*

But mostly, the question is an acknowledgement that a lot has changed in four years. The average Obama supporter is no longer in wide-eyed wonderment over the prospects of electing our first black president - four years after history was made, many of us are still grappling with the socio-economic ravages of Bush Administration policies, and confounded over what seems to be President Obama's commitment to adhering to some of the most unpopular of them – Guantanamo Bay is still open; we've expanded what has been a costly presence in Afghanistan under President Obama, and he's failed up till now to end the Bush-era tax cuts given to the wealthiest Americans and corporations, despite the fact that the nation's debt and budget deficit continue to skyrocket, and our social safety nets are on the verge of collapse. It's just a fact - whatever their race, many of the President's supporters find themselves disappointed in the wake of what have been characterized as broken promises made during the 2008 election, and there are those on the left that have been vocal about their belief that President Obama has given up too much in tough fights with Republicans these last few years.

Even a rabid Obama supporter like me can admit that there have been some disappointing moments in his presidency. I question the wisdom, for example of expending vast amounts of his political capital on waging a long and protracted healthcare reform fight, only to end up with legislation that as of this writing, is being challenged constitutionally before the Supreme Court, legislation that did not go nearly far enough to protect the nation's citizens in a way that almost every other industrialized country in the world has been able to. I understood the rationale then, and I understand it now - tackle the sector of our economy that seems most intractable, and that is in the most danger of destroying our nation's ability to *sustain* a healthy economy and more importantly, a healthy citizenry for the future – I get it.

The need for reform was even more important in light of the fact that Baby Boomers, who outnumber every other age group in the nation, are approaching retirement, and in danger of completely overwhelming the healthcare system as we know it now if we don't get costs under control. Again, I get it, and you probably do too. But waging that fight at a time when the country was literally hemorrhaging jobs that have been too slow to come back, and the fact that it all may have been for naught if the Conservatives on the Supreme Court have their way, can't help but make even the President's biggest supporters wonder what he and his advisors were thinking.

So it's 2012, and even I, the original Black Woman for Obama have to ask myself the question: *are you in?*

It's not as easy a question for me to answer as it might seem. It's not just about *will I vote for President Obama* – of course I will. The question for me and others like me is *will I work myself into the ground again to fight for his re-election?* As one of the pseudo leaders of the original volunteer corps, will I shut down a large part of my life once more to go out and make sure that as many people in the nation as possible work to get President Obama re-elected, give more blood, sweat, tears, time, and money? Has he earned it?

In my opinion? Yes. Actually, hell yes. And I'll tell you why. Feel me on this one for a moment.

Several months ago, Melissa Harris-Perry, the brilliant college professor and MSNBC show host did a segment on the *Rachel Maddow* show called the *Tale of Two Michelle's*, where she talked about the disparities inherent in the way the media (at the time) treated Michelle Obama versus how they treated Michelle Bachmann during her failed run for the Republican nomination. It so happens that I have my own two-tales story. I call it – "The Tale of Two Shovels"

The Tale of Two Shovels

So, imagine there's a job – everyone wants it. And to do this job, you have to be good at doing two things – digging a hole, and filling it back up with dirt – that's it. Dig the hole and then fill it back up with dirt. The thing is – you have to dig this hole in such a way that the one that comes after you, can always either a) start the digging where you left off or b) begin to fill the hole where you left off. Simple, right?

Now imagine that you get this job – from what you've heard, every one of your predecessors, from the beginning of time, has dug the hole, oh, maybe 5, six feet deep, and worked like crazy to fill it back in. You're not nervous – you know you're going to have to dig a little, or toss a little dirt in, and you're up for the task. Well - imagine your surprise, when (upon reporting for duty your first day of work, shovel in hand), you find that the guy that had the job *before you*, has dug a hole 100 feet deep, and left it for you to fill. Oh – and you have no idea where the dirt is. You still only have 5 feet worth of dirt to fill the hole in with.

In essence – your predecessor has thrown his shovel down, flipped you the bird on the way out, and ran back to his ranch in Texas, I mean, back to wherever he came from, leaving you to deal with the bizarre results of his efforts. And now, not only are your co-workers pressuring you to fill in the hole, those folks who want the job after you are *yelling* for you to fill the hole. Everyone everywhere wants you to fill in the hole. Fill in the damned hole! Do it now! Yikes.

You try to reason with them - "my predecessor dug a MUCH bigger hole than he should have, a-and there's no more dirt with which to fill it kind people!", and they tell you to shut your trap – less yapping, more hole management! Enough about your predecessor, it's YOUR hole now, and *you* have to find a way to fill it with dirt. And you better not complain.

Get the picture? President Obama took office at an historic time for America and the world; 700,000 plus jobs were exiting the economy each month; our auto industry was on the verge of collapse, and in danger of taking another one million jobs with it; the financial institutions in this country were disintegrating in the wake of too much greed and too little regulation and because of an expensive and unjust war in Iraq, our reputation around the world was in tatters – when President Obama took the oath of office, he had been left with a very deep hole to fill indeed.

And yet – here we are four years later, arguably through the worst of the last big recession, with an auto industry that's back on top around the world, and with an economy that has added 200,000 new jobs each of the last three months. This is of course not to say that Americans are no longer feeling the pain of the recession, but it can definitely be argued that as a result of Obama's leadership and his administration's policies, a lot of the magical, disappearing dirt has made its way back into the hole. So yes – I'm in. And you should be too.

I believed back in 2008, and I believe now that President Obama is a leader for this time; even as we debate policies, and distill critical issues into 30-second sound bites, there are important realities that we face as a nation, realities that I believe have informed the President's policies, and which are as important and impactful today as they were then. I call them "the three shuns":

Globalization. The harsh truth that many don't want to face is that our ability to conduct commerce across shores easily and seamlessly due to technology means that there are many, many jobs that have left this country that are never coming back. Period. Competing tax rates aside, there are just too many countries with cheap, plentiful labor who are willing and able to do the work Americans used to do, and who *can* now, thanks to the internet and other communications technologies that make doing business across thousands of miles feel like doing business across the hall.

Education. America is not educating its citizens adequately to compete in the recently mentioned Global Economy. According to a study done by the 2009 Programme for International Student Assessment released in 2010, 15-year-old students in the U.S.

perform about average in reading and science, and below average in math. Out of 34 countries, the U.S. ranked 14th in reading, 17th in science and 25th in math. And even as unemployment continues to hover around 8.1 percent, many jobs that require high-tech skills are going unfilled and leaving companies no choice but to look outside our borders for the workers they need.

Innovation. In every major recession since recessions have been recorded, it's taken some major innovation to spur the country back into economic health. The commercialization of the Internet helped fuel economic recovery after the recession of the early 90's, for example - innovation has facilitated the kind of economic expansion that results in periods of growth that are typically longer than the recession itself. But innovation takes a level of commitment that the nation has lost, and as a result, countries are cleaning our clocks when it comes to keeping up with our infrastructure, and investing in alternate forms of energy.

And I'm convinced that President Obama understands all of this, and that he has tried over the last three-and-a-half years (with debatable success), to manage the country to those realities always, with shovel in hand, trying to restore order to the hole.

And so as I look back on what's been since my time as an Obama volunteer, and think about what's to come, I can honestly say that no – this time, there will likely not be the tingles that ran up and down my and Chris Matthews' legs during the last election; there may not be the adoring, impassioned crowds, the t-shirts and theme songs, or the plentiful celebrity spokespeople. And worst of all, there may not be the fired up, engaged volunteer corps that helped propel the President into office. So that's where *Black Women for Obama* comes in. It's our job *this time* to cut through the rhetoric, and the bias, and to spread the message of his real record – the record that includes passing the *Lily Ledbetter Act* to give woman equal pay for an equal days work; a record that includes more financial reforms meant to protect average Americans than ever before in history, and an expansion of environmental policies that rivals any recent President. And a record that shows an ability to go after and defeat our enemies, in ways that actually make us safer as a nation, without all the lip service.

I'm in – I'm still a Black Woman for Obama. I believe in what the next four years will bring, and I believe in the President's ability to bring it. So I hope you'll come on in too – the political waters are fine.